The MIKE MEN of TRINIDAD & TOBAGO

By **Dr. Primnath Gooptar**

with an introduction by Professor Brinsley Samaroo

THE MIKE MEN OF TRINIDAD & TOBAGO

By: Primnath Gooptar (Ph.D.)

75 Green Street, Tunapuna

Trinidad, West Indies.

Email: pgoopta@hotmail.com

Published 2020

ISBN:

Appreciation

The author thanks the Mike Men Association of Trinidad and Tobago, and all those interviewed for the project for their support in producing this historical document on the mike men of Trinidad and Tobago. Those quoted in this book include Anderson Bahaw, Balliram Ramoutar, Darren Basdeo, Dianand Balgobin, Dipchand Maharaj (deceased), Doeraj Harrikissoon (deceased), Gary Dassawh, Harrypersad Harrikissoon, Hublal Ramkissoon, Imtiaz Ali, Ishmael Hoosaney, James Ramnath (deceased), John Jagroopsingh (deceased), Krishna Timol, Mulchan Singh, Nanlal Ramcharan (deceased), Narsaloo Ramaya (deceased), Partap Sitahal, Pickrani Gooptar, Ralph Narine (deceased), Ramdeowar Ramjattan (deceased), Ramesh Boodhoo (deceased), Randy Kissoon, Ranjit Singh, Ricky Harrypersad, Rooplal Boodlal, Shaheed Mohammed, Siew Gosine (deceased), Siew Lalchan, Sonia Maharaj.

Pictures: Anderson Bahaw, Darren Basdeo, Dianand Balgobin, Primnath Gooptar, Ricky Harrypersad, Shaheed Mohammed.

Introduction: Professor Emeritus Brinsley Samaroo
Editor: Devika Cassandra Gooptar (Ph.D.)

Note from the author:

This book was inspired by a paper which I originally presented at a conference in Paramaribo, Suriname on the Legacy of Slavery and Indentured Labour,

6 - 10 June, 2013

The words mike, funnels and horns, as used in this book, convey the same meaning and are used interchangeably.

Dedication

This book is dedicated

to the Mike Men of Trinidad and Tobago

who helped to preserve and propagate

Indian culture through their

hard work in the

rural areas

of the

country.

CONTENTS

Message from Deoroop Teemal:

Independent Senator, Parliament of Trinidad & Tobago; First Vice President, National Council of Indian Culture (NCIC); Chairman, NCIC Heritage Centre.

DEOROOP TEEMAL

There are times when a culture is guilty of taking for granted movements that have shaped and contributed significantly to its growth and development in unique, distinct and intangible ways. In my opinion, this is the case with the mike men and their incomparable role in the promotion and propagation of Indian culture in Trinidad & Tobago. The mike men evolved from the heart and needs of the community and through their high degree of indigenous innovation and creativity, evolved to fulfil the sound and music needs at Indian weddings, religious events, funerals, festivals and community events as well becoming the mainstay for the sole dissemination of information through community announcements, for a prolonged period of time. Through sheer determination, they carved a distinct space in the Indian cultural landscape and went on to become an integral and valued element of this landscape.

From humble beginnings in the early days of their trade, the mike man eventually rose to play a vital and sometimes dominant role in Indian cultural events. The trade of the mike man evolved from the back seat of cars that had seen better days along with an assembly of low-brand horns, turntables and amplifiers powered by the car battery, all put together by enthusiasts with no formal training in sound engineering and production. As the author has clearly identified in the book, the rise of the popularity of Hindi film songs saw a decline in the popularity of nautanki dance dramas such as the Raja Harischandra and the Indar Sabha performed at the cooking/farewell nights of the Hindu wedding as well as the local classical singing that formed part of the entertainment for those attending. This provided the opportune slot for the mike men who took full advantage to cement their place within this event and become a cherished and appreciated part of wedding proceedings eventually being given the honour of leading the wedding procession, signalling to the village the departure of the bridegroom to the bride's home and his subsequent arrival back home with his new bride.

We are also familiar with having our late evenings or early nights interrupted on occasions by mike announcements informing of deaths within the village and those of adjacent villages, funeral arrangements, invitations to attend yajnas, community events and other public announcements. The image of two horns mounted on a moving car with the operator in the back seat who somehow manages to keep the turntable steady as the vinyl records are spun on it, will continue to fill us with wonder.

Another marked feature of the mike men is the sense of camaraderie and brotherhood that has grown amongst their fraternity through the competitive and friendly sound clashes or sound offs. They have managed to create a forum where they get together to enjoy each other's company, take pride in their trade and advance their craft to higher standards of performance. The advent of the Indian orchestras and the big box DJ's have tempered the role and importance of the mike man to some extent but they will continue to be relevant in the Indian cultural landscape as they continue to find ways to ply their trade despite these challenges.

This book is a signal effort in documentation of the cultural history of Trinidad & Tobago. Dr. Primnath Gooptar must be commended for choosing to document this important but often overlooked aspect of our culture. Most importantly, he has painstakingly interviewed the persons involved from the lens of a cultural insider and this has resulted in an emphatic and honest discourse on the subject matter. In this book, Dr. Gooptar has managed to successfully capture the aspirations and the factors shaping the development of the mike men and the relevant role they have played in the promotion of Indian culture in Trinidad & Tobago.

Independent Senator
DEOROOP TEEMAL

Message from the Trinidad and Tobago Mobile Paging Association

RANDY KISSOON

(This message was penned by Randy Kissoon in 2017 when this project started. He was at the time president of the Trinidad and Tobago Mobile Paging Association which later became the Mike Men Association of Trinidad and Tobago.)

On behalf of the mike men of Trinidad, I feel very privileged to present this message, and in doing so, I wish to congratulate Dr. Gooptar on this valuable initiative of recording the history of the mike men in Trinidad and Tobago. This book, I am confident, would be classified as a historical document in the annals of the history of this country.

The mike man emerged in this country in the 1940s and carved a niche for themselves by dint of their hard work, dedication and integrity. They traveled the length and breadth of this country with their portable public address systems attached to their motor cars, bringing joy and happiness to thousands of people across the land, all of whom loved to hear the Indian film songs.

In the early days, the mike men were fashionable at Indian weddings, bazaars, chathies, barahies and other such occasions and it was their willingness to please their audiences that endeared them to the people with whom they came into contact. Wherever he went, in those days, the mike man was a veritable star boy in his own right, and everyone wanted to befriend him or make requests for him to play their favourite songs.

As time went by and the music box systems became widespread and Indian orchestras ruled the stage at cooking nights, the visibility of the mike man at those events declined. However, he remained an integral part of the society, still carrying the Indian weddings on Sundays, making death announcements, announcements for community events such as Ramayan Yaagnas and Bhagwat Yaagnas, school bazaars and other such activities. In addition, his services are employed by politicians in their election campaigns and by several businesses to announce their goods and services. As the mike man continued to function in the society, he found ways to move on and to modify his systems in ways that the early mike men had never imagined.

This new breed of mike men can spend between $50,000-$70,000 to modify their systems for competitive purposes. I can liken this to a motor car being prepared for a competition. Just as a motor car is modified for competitions, so too, amplifiers and the mike systems are modified for competitions. These modified systems are not used in making routine announcements. At the back of all this is the work of the mike technicians who work behind the scenes to modify those systems to make them competitive units. Without the work of the technicians, the mike man could not produce the kind of systems required for the 'sound-off' competitions. Every year, there are a few sound-off competitions where trophies are awarded to the best mike man, but the main event remains our Indian Arrival Day sound-off competition where there are several categories for the mike men to present their 'work of art.'

There are over 250 mike men in this country, and they are represented by the Mike Men Association of Trinidad and Tobago, which continues to make representation on their behalf. This organization continues to hold the mike men together as a unit, to share commonalities and create camaraderieship among them. Every Sunday, these mike men gather at the Preysal Recreation Ground in friendly banter and sound-off clashes as they pit their systems against each other.

I believe that the mike men will be here for a long time to come, and as they continue to evolve in this society, they will find innovative ways to continue their work and their hobby as mike men.

Message from the Mike Men Association of Trinidad and Tobago

ANAND KISSOON
(President)

I have the opportunity to serve as President of the Mikemen Association of Trinidad and Tobago for the years 2019 and 2020.

This organization was previously known as Trinidad and Tobago Mobile Paging Association. As mikemen we remain eager and optimistic about our future by "Keeping our community informed, educated and entertained."

We are proud to serve the public for the past years and we will continue to do so in the future. We are a member association and our aim is to be an agile organization that responds to the need of our members.

The mike men have been an integral part of Trinidad and Tobago society since the 1940s and played an important role in the evolution of Indian culture and communication in T&T.

We commend Dr. Gooptar for taking the time to research the work of the mike men in Trinidad and present it to the public. It is our hope that this book will assist the public in a better understanding of the mike men of yesteryear and today.

INTRODUCTION

**Professor Emeritus
Brinsley Samaroo**

For all of 72 years until 1917, Indians were transported over 12,000 miles from one side of the world to the other under the Indian indentureship system. In the majority of cases, those who came never went back, but were left to re-construct their lives after the deconstruction wrought by the traumas of crossing the *kala pani*. To their advantage, however, these Indians had come from a high civilization with a value system created over thousands of years. So, although they were illiterate in Western languages, they connected with each other in their own languages and culture and consoled themselves by reliance on the scriptures which they had brought from India. On the ships they were allowed to bring basic instruments such as their dholak (drums), harmonium and cymbals. From 1935, with the introduction of the first Indian film, Bala Joban, there followed a long line of other films. Since then, Indian filmi music has become part of the local culture as these presented a way of life that had been gradually fading away. However, these Indian films were mainly shown in urban areas such as Port of Spain, San Fernando and Couva. Rural folks had to travel long distances to get to these venues, braving rain and bad roads, investing too much time and money in that exercise. However, the craving for at least the music persisted. In that scenario, a group of brave, risk-taking men came to the rescue by becoming mike men.

The mike men were innovators in that they played the traditional filmi music from Indian playback singers such as Mohammed Rafi, Lata Mangeshkar, Hemant Kumar, Mukesh, Asha Bhonsle and Manna Dey. In this way, the mike then became *Ustads* (musical masters) in their own right. They banded together to create a viable organization, established branches in various communities in Central and South Trinidad and expanded their activities as they became increasingly popular. As Ramdeowar recounts in this book, he was a mike man for some six decades and he enjoyed the job immensely. He remembered that women ran out of their houses with dough on their hands as they lined the roads to see the mike man who he became the center of attraction, like the star boy himself. Soon the mike men were hired to play for days on end at weddings and other festive occasions. Commercial establishments used them for advertising their goods and then came the politicians who, at election time, hired the mike men for extended periods. At times of death, the mike men became the carriers of information about funeral arrangements.

Being a mike man carried other advantages. Romantic alliances were formed with village women and everyone enjoyed the competitive clashes among groups of mike men. In these many ways, the mike men emerged as *deeyas* in darkened villages where entertainment was limited. As upholders of Indian culture, they fulfilled a cultural need which was deeply felt by those who had come from afar and felt abandoned on the sugar estates which were concerned only with their labour. Today they continue to fulfil that role, but in a more sophisticated way with better equipment and modern technology. The author of this book spent years in the field meeting mike men and their followers who found comfort in the endeavors of these artistes. Life in our rural communities would have been much bleaker without these Mike Men who have functioned as custodians of Indo-culture. The book is clearly written, properly illustrated with rare photographs and easily readable by the general population.

Professor Emeritus Brinsley Samaroo
Department of History
The University of the West Indies
St. Augustine Campus

CHAPTER 1

The Arrival of the Mike Men

"In the tiny Caribbean island of Trinidad and Tobago, there is a community of Indians known as the mike men. They are a group of males cultishly devoted to automobile borne amplification. Each of their cars has two enormous air raid warning megaphones attached to its roof."[1] The Mike Men of Trinidad.

Horns were the earliest form of sound amplification used by man. From the earliest times, what were referred to as horn instruments or funnels, most likely derived its name, and were obtained from, the horns of sheep, cows or other wild animals. Since antiquity, those natural horns were used to amplify sound for various purposes and may be the oldest known device for amplifying sound.

The power of the sound and its amplification through the horn has been recognized for thousands of years and was used to good effect in palaces, in cities, and in wars. The amplified sound, through the horn, often interrupted the sound-scape of the city or the battlefields and played an imperative role in calling attention to the public or to soldiers in the Army for a specific action.

This was especially so since the human voice was insufficient or incapable of drawing attention to a wide span of people.

The evolution of the horn as an instrument to magnify sound, especially the human voice, gained momentum with the invention of the phonograph.

A view of several types of external gramophone horns

---

1   http://www.facebook.com/pages/themikemen...
The mike men's website mike men of Trinidad description of the mike and the mike men:

An early home gramophone in Trinidad

Mike Systems bolted on to the hood of motor vehicles, Trinidad.

Horns were then added to the device to amplify the sound emanating from the disc spinner.

Horns became a fundamental appendage of the early gramophones to increase the intensity of the sound produced by the mechanical sound apparatus. Later, by the 1920s, they were used in radios, public address systems and theater sound systems because they gave a more extensive public coverage.

Early phonographs and gramophones in Trinidad used the horn system to amplify the music played through those apparatuses.
By the late 1920s, there were wooden box systems used to amplify sounds in public gatherings. The first horn or funnel mike system was imported into Trinidad in the 1930s, but there was limited public usage.[2] However, with improvements, by the 1940s, their public use increased, and they became widespread as 'announcers,' used mainly to amplify voices and songs.

Initially, these mike systems were considered 'loud and noisy instruments' because of the sheer power with which they blasted sound all around. People in the country, particularly those from the wealthy upper class, had not previously experienced such high levels of loud music in public spaces, and many considered the instruments a public nuisance.

Mike systems as a significant roving communication device in Trinidad have been used for decades by local rural broadcast entrepreneurs, who bought these ensembles and journeyed through the countryside playing music to entertain the masses. These mike systems are some of the most powerful amplification sound systems, and their sounds can be heard for miles around. The operators of those systems are called *mike men* who, by the 1970s, formed an organization to represent their interests.

Brief History of the Mike Men Association

In discussing the origins of the Mike Men Association, Harrypersad Harrikissoon, a mike man for over thirty years now residing in the USA explained: "There have been several incarnations of the Mike Men Association under different names. The first coming together of the mike men began in 1971. The mike men at the time formed themselves into the *Trinidad and Tobago Mike Association* with Kamalodeen Mohammed as the legal advisor and his nephew, Solo Latiff, being the 1st president of the organization. Even then, we met and pitched our mikes against each other in friendly clashes. It is important to note that in those days, the Association negotiated permits for the mike men to play their mike systems on the roads of Trinidad and Tobago. The permits were usually granted on an annual basis and had to be renewed each year."

In consonance with the views of Harripersad, Randy Kissoon noted that the coming together of the mike men in the 1970s was an important milestone for the mike men of Trinidad as the association brought together mike men from different parts of the country and helped to create a sense of camaraderie among them. He continued, "That is not to say that before the advent of the Mike Association many of them did not share records or experiences, but the

---

2   Ramjattan Ramdeowar.

Mike Men Association of Trinidad and Tobago New Executive (2020/2021). From left to Right: the President Anand Kissoon, Vice President Anand Boxer, Secretary Gary Dassawh, Assistant Secretary Shaheed Mohammed, Committee Member Rabindranath Persad, PRO Premnath Ramnath, Committee Member Shafeer Mohammed. Back Row: Vinod Persad Maharaj, Treasurer Gopaul Ramsamooj, Anderson Bahaw Jagjit Ramrattan and Shaheed Mohammed.

coming together under the umbrella of the Mike Association, encouraged several mike men who had never met each other, and who had only known of others through their mike names, to develop relationships that lasted for years."

In early 2000, Hublal Ramkissoon aka *Boy* took over the reins of leadership of the organization which by that time had undergone a change in name and was registered with the Ministry of Community Development. The new name of the organization was *Trinidad and Tobago Mobile Paging Association*. In 2012

Randy Kissoon became its new president and held that post until 2019. According to Gary Dassawh, Secretary of the Association, in 2019, there was another name change and a new organization was registered with the Ministry of Community Development, Culture and Arts under the name of *The Mike Men Association of Trinidad and Tobago*. He indicated that the organization meets once every month and holds its Annual General Elections in February-March each year. Dassawh further revealed that the association also organizes several fund-raising events such as raffles, Family Days, Sports Days, All Fours matches, Sound-off competitions and the friendly Sunday sound-off clashes. The major Sound-off competition is the Annual Indian Arrival Day Sound-off Contest. At all the Sound-off competitions there are a number of categories and trophies are presented to the first, second and third place winners in each category.

Mike Systems

A mike system is a roving public address arrangement consisting of two large funnel-shaped horns, horn drivers, an amplifier, a motor car battery, a backup battery, a turntable (portable record player) that plays 78 RPM vinyl records

The long neck and short neck horns

and a microphone. The huge horns are attached to the roof of an automobile with a hood rack system while the other attachments are placed inside the vehicle during 'mike' operations.

Dianand Balgobin, in explaining the working of the system, noted, "the record player sends a signal to the amplifier, and the amplifier magnifies that sound and sends it to the driver units attached to the funnels, and the sound comes out through the funnels. Inside each driver unit, there is a diaphragm that vibrates with the frequency of the sound. Sometimes these diaphragms may rupture and are destroyed because of the extremely loud or high-intensity sound coming from the amplifier, and they have to be replaced. The technicians help to balance these factors, so the driver units do not blow." [3]

Despite the increasing cost of maintaining the mike systems, these mike men have continued to keep their systems in excellent working conditions.

---

3   Dianand Balgobin. Telephone interview. Tableland. 18/10/19

Two Types of Mike Systems

Randy Kissoon, former president of the Trinidad and Tobago Mobile Paging Association and considered by many mike men, one of the most experienced mike men in the business, noted there are two types of mike systems operated by mike men in this country. One is the regular, average long neck mike system used for announcements and for playing at weddings and other social events. The other mike ensemble he characterized as; "a high-end short neck mike system upgraded and modified for competitive purposes. As a comparison, the regular mike system can cost from $10,000-$15,000 on average while a high-end competitive system can be produced from between $40,000 to $55,000. These prices may vary depending on what the mike man requires and what may be needed to complete the system. I have heard some mike man quote prices of $60,000-$70,000, but that again is an individual matter." [4]

However, in the early days of the mike men in Trinidad, there was just the ordinary long neck mike system that were used at Indian weddings and various other events, mostly in the Indian communities. It was at the Indian weddings that the mike men found a niche in the market that propelled them into national prominence.

---

[4]   Randy Kissoon. Personal Interview, Cunupia. 15/5/2017

CHAPTER 2

The Mike Men and Hindu Weddings

"The cooking nights of the fifties and sixties, when a mike man played there, were the best days of the mike men. He emerged as the star attraction at the cooking nights playing Indian film songs and thus became a cultural icon for East Indians. I sometimes wish that we could see a return to those days when the mike man could go into the wedding tents and play for the entire session." Imtiaz Ali.

Until the mid-1950s, Hindu weddings were all-night affairs commencing at 6 p.m. and ending at 6 a.m. the next morning. After 1955, the Hindu night weddings were gradually phased out, and such marriages took place during the daytime, usually on a Sunday. Entertainment at Hindu weddings before the 1950s consisted mostly of classical singing and dance dramas, which lasted through the night. There were no sound amplification systems available in those early years, and singers and actors in the dance dramas strained their voices to the maximum to be heard over the often noisy and boisterous wedding attendees.

Wedding affairs in those days were very open events, and everyone in the village attended, whether invited or not. With the advent of the mike systems in the country, Hindu wedding hosts employed the mike men to amplify the voices of the classical singers and the dance-drama personnel. There was only one microphone attached to the amplifier and that microphone was passed from one person to the other as needed. This amplification of sound at the Hindu wedding was a novelty for East Indians, and the popularity of the mike man gradually spread among members of the East Indian community. As his reputation grew among the wedding gatherings, he was commonly referred to as 'the mike man' because his primary purpose for being at the weddings was to use the microphone to amplify the voices of actors and singers. Hence, due to regular use and for quick reference, the term microphone was shortened to 'mike.' John Jagroopsingh, a cultural enthusiast, indicated that as the mike man arrived at locations where he played, members of the public were heard to remark, 'the mike man reach,' 'look the mike come,' 'the mike passing (meaning going by),' 'mike man play (name of a favourite song) for meh,' all referring to the man with the microphone.[5]

In time, the operator of the microphone came to be known as the 'mike man.' The term 'mike man' passed into common usage and came to refer to the

<hr>

5 John Jagroopsingh Personal Interview. Brazil Village, Arima.14/11/17

operators of the horn amplifier systems. Soon, the word 'mike' also came to refer to the large horns or funnels placed on the hood of automobiles, and people pointed to the horns when referring to the mike. Thus, the term 'mike,' which initially alluded to the microphone, came to refer to the horns and later to the entire system. The name 'mike man,' which at first depicted the man 'operating' (handling) the microphone, came to refer to the owner of the mike system or the man operating the turntable, which was usually the same person.

The mike men made their most significant impact on East Indians at Hindu weddings, where they continually played Indian film songs. It was here that the mike men found a niche for themselves and, in the process, became identified with Indian film songs as their main menu.

When East Indians came to Trinidad as indentured immigrants, they worked in the cane fields almost every day. There were very few free days for weddings or religious celebrations, so their weddings were held at night, usually on a Saturday night. By the 1950s, because of 'disturbances' at the night weddings, some pundits began to shift the Hindu wedding celebration to a Sunday. By the 1960s, the daytime Hindu marriage had become the norm and continues to the present.

During the early years of the mike man at the Hindu night wedding ceremonies, there were breaks or intervals during the official entertainment programme (which consisted of classical singing and dance dramas), and the mike man made use of the intervals at those events to play Indian film songs.

The regular entertainment menu at the night weddings consisted of traditional songs, local Indian classical singing, and dance dramas such as the Raja Harischandra and Indra Sabha dances. In the case of the Raja Harischandra dance-drama, which ran from 8 p.m. until 6 a.m. the next morning, there were blank periods, during which time the artists took a rest or prepared for the next session. The mike men seized those opportunities to keep the audiences entertained with Indian film songs played through their mike systems, much to the delight of wedding audiences. In this way, he popularized Indian film songs at Hindu weddings.

East Indians loved the Indian film songs because they were very catchy, rhythmic, and melodious, and many people enjoyed listening to those songs through the mike systems during these intervals at the wedding nights. Soon, audiences demanded the playing of Indian cinema songs for longer intervals at the wedding nights, and people looked forward to the playing of the film songs on the mike system during such extended intervals. Some people went to those night weddings and waited for hours for those intervals when the mike man played Indian film songs. [6] As audience demands for the mike man grew at the Hindu night weddings, he began arriving early at those events and entertained the first arrivals with his Indian film songs, from as early as 5 p.m.

---

[6] Interview with Nanlal Ramcharan .Plum Road, Sangre Grande; 08/04/09 and Ramjattan Ramdeowar. Personal Interview, St. Augustine. 12/05/08

until the classical singers and dance performers took over the entertainment proceedings later in the evening. In addition, he continued playing at intervals during the night. On occasions, at the Hindu night weddings, there were disappointments with the nonappearance of the dance-drama troupe or the classical singers, and the mike man was asked to fill in the entertainment gap.

Siew Gosine, Indar Sabha and Raja Harischandra dancer.

This, he did willingly and much to the delight of the fans in the audience. Many people, particularly the wedding hosts, were surprised that in such emergencies, the mike man 'carried' the entire wedding night playing Indian film songs for the enjoyment of the audience.

During the classical singing sessions and the dance-drama performances at wedding nights, many young people took very little interest in the events of the night; it was the opposite whenever the mike man played Indian film songs. Most people remained to hear the mike songs, and on the special occasions when he played for the entire night at the Hindu wedding, everyone stayed for the whole night, enjoyed the songs, and kept asking for more. What started, therefore, as a stopgap measure to fill in for an absent troupe or a group of singers, caught the attention of everyone, and by the mid-1950s, the mike man was the preferred form of entertainment at Hindu weddings. The classical singers and the dance-drama groups were gradually pushed into the background, and by the late 1970s, there were very few Indian dance-drama groups in the country.

Siew Gosine, an Indar Sabha and Raja Harischandra dancer explained: "We were called out to put on our play at many celebrations such as the sixth day or the twelfth-day observances of the birth of a child; birthday celebrations and wedding nights. At the Hindu wedding night celebration, we saw our biggest crowds. Our play went on for the whole night, but there were breaks in between when we took a little rest and prepared for the next scene. In earlier times, a few classical singers were brought in to fill those gaps, but then as time went by, the mike system came in and assisted us. I must tell you that in the early days, there was no mike for us to speak to the audience, so we usually spoke with a loud voice so that the audience would hear us. I think it was somewhere in the late 1940s that these mike men were hired to provide loudspeakers, so we used to use the mike to talk. I can still recall the first time I held the mike in my hand. I was frightened like hell. I was very nervous as I had never talked on the mike before. I almost dropped the mike. After a while, I got accustomed to it and actually looked forward to using the mike during our presentations.

Like I told you during the break time, these mike men played some of the most beautiful Indian movie songs you would ever hear. I enjoyed them and sometimes wished that they would not stop, but then we had to put on our play, and they had to stop playing to give us a chance to continue with our dance-drama. Now, remember we were the stars of the night, and the mike man was only there to support us. As I said, they played the Indian film songs, and after a few years I observed, we, the Harischandra dancers, discovered that people began to 'much up' the mike men more than us who were supposed to be the stars of the night. I can tell you what I noticed during those days. Many people came to the wedding night celebrations, and when we did our act, there was a fair amount of people in the tents. Within an hour, many of those people had left and gone outside either to take a smoke or to lime, but when the mike man played, they all came back in and filled up the tent. When he stopped, we returned to put on our dance-drama, and a good few people just went back outside. The funny thing was that in our case people needed to see us doing our dance-drama because we had costumes and so on but the mike was very loud, and they could hear it clearly from the outside, but as soon as the mike man started up they came back in to 'see ' him in action while they ignored us and went outside while we acted. In a few years, there was a reversal of roles as the mike man became the main attraction for the night and we were just given a few short periods to perform our acts." [7]

On the same note, Ramjattan Ramdeowar who had been a mike man for over 60 years, also added; "Sometimes, in those early days of the 1950s, when I went to play at the night weddings, I did not too much like to play there because I did not think that we were very much appreciated in those early days. Some people said that we were too noisy while others felt that using the mike during their dance dramas was a humbug, and some of them refused to use the mike outright because they said that their voices were loud enough. But I did not mind much because we were being paid to do a job, but it sometimes hurt when people said we were too noisy. I remember I went to do a wedding right here in St. Augustine over the highway when a woman who lived nearby came

<hr>

[7]   Siew Gosine. Personal Interview, Mundo Nuevo.18/03/09

to the wedding tent and shouted at me, saying I was making too much noise in the neighborhood and she could not sleep.

"Anyway, back to what you wanted to know. Yes, sometimes, some classical singers and dance-drama people refused to use the mike because they felt that their voices were louder than the mike. They were jokers. My mike was one of the loudest, and people heard it for more than three miles around…

"As I said, I did not like very much to play when the dance dramas were put on at the wedding nights because I could not shine with my records. I paid

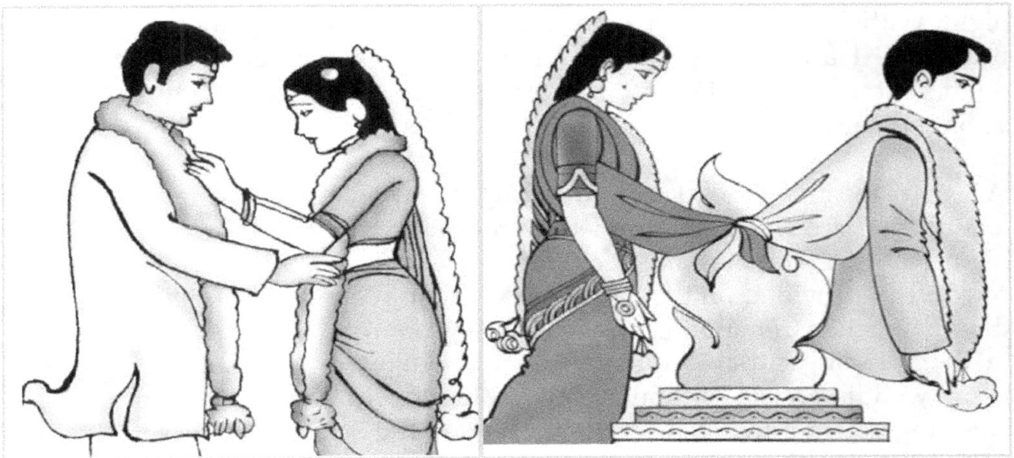

Scenes at a Hindu wedding.

good money to buy my 78 records (vinyl records), and when we went there, I was just given a few short periods to play my songs, and sometimes the drama dancers did not even want to use the microphone. I think in many cases, they feared using the microphone. One time I also asked one dancer if he thought the mike would bite him, and they all laughed. But I can tell you one thing that when we played, even for the short times, everyone there enjoyed our songs and did not want us to stop.

I played good music. Those film songs were very catchy, and many people loved them. I think the playing of film songs on the loud mike system in those days was a novelty for many people attending the wedding nights, but I do not believe that the people paying us recognized that. On a few occasions, I mentioned to my wedding host to give me a little more time to play my records and although I was given a little extra time they all remarked that they did not want to upset the dance-drama people, so they had to allow them enough time to put on their play. You had to be there to feel the atmosphere. People wanted to hear us play the mike instead of watching the dance-drama. Sometimes, it almost came to blows as people booed the dance-drama people off the stage saying we 'want the song, we want to hear songs.' But the dance-drama was a big thing in those days, and so they were allowed to continue. However, little by little, people demanded more of the music and less of the dance-drama, until the Saturday cooking night became our major stomping ground where we were in control and played our mike to the fullest. Wherever there was a wedding, and in those days, Hindu marriages were held on Sundays, we played from Saturday night until Sunday evening, and people came from all around to listen to us. Those were the glory days of the mike men, and we were the stars in the cooking night." [8]

In the initial wedding arrangements, pre-1950s, because the wedding was generally held on a Saturday night, certain prenuptial ceremonies (Hardi) were performed on the night preceding the wedding, which was usually a Friday night. With the shift of the wedding ceremonies to the Sunday (daytime), the prenuptial Hardi rituals could have been brought forward to the Saturday night, but most people kept the tradition of the Friday night prenuptial arrangements.

When, by the mid-1950s, Hindu weddings became a daytime affair, usually on a Sunday, there was a vacuum left on the Saturday night between the Friday night Hardi ceremonies and the Sunday wedding rituals. The entertainment previously provided on the Saturday wedding night was mainly to entertain the bhaaraatians (visitors) from the bridegroom's entourage. With the shift in the wedding rituals from the Saturday night to the Sunday (daytime), many wedding hosts continued the tradition of entertainment for the visiting entourage during the wedding ceremony on the Sunday. However, this was not very practical as there were concerns that the entertainment was a cause of disruption when the wedding rituals were being performed. For many people, a Hindu wedding was an excuse for elaborate entertainment and socialization, so more people preferred to pay attention to the entertainment taking place than the wedding rituals. As a result, in many instances, the extravagant Sunday entertainment at Hindu weddings gradually diminished, and the Saturday night entertainment became the norm.

Now wedding ceremonies among the East Indians were known "open affairs," and villagers, friends, families, and well-wishers always assisted the wedding hosts with cash donations or foodstuffs. At the time when such weddings were held at nights, villagers, friends, and relatives supported the hosts and cooked and fed all visitors. This feeding of attendees went on throughout the night.

When the wedding was shifted to the Sunday daytime, many wedding hosts kept the tradition of cooking and feeding guests and visitors during the wedding day (Sunday). However, there were difficulties with concluding the cooking chores on time, especially the preparation of the roti. To resolve the problem, many wedding hosts prepared some of the food items during the 'free' Saturday night. Friends and relatives were invited to keep company with the cooks as they prepared food items (mainly roti) for the next day while others prepared various talkaries (vegetable dishes) for cooking on the Sunday. To keep the attendees 'lively and entertained,' people told stories, jokes and danced and sang among themselves. Eventually, as the Saturday night gatherings grew, the dance dramas and classical singers were once again invited to provide entertainment. As the event took on new proportions, and the people joined in, not just to keep company with the cooks, but to enjoy the entertainment, the Saturday night event mushroomed into a hugely popular event which came to be called the 'cooking night.' The mike man was an integral part of that evolution and from the mid-1950s to the late 1980s, he became the preferred choice of entertainment at thousands of cooking nights throughout the country. So, what began as entertainment to keep family, friends, well-wishers, and the cooks in good spirits during the cooking nights turned out to be a significant event at Hindu weddings.

Often, the Saturday cooking night entertainment eclipsed the actual wedding day event as many people preferred to attend the cooking night because of the entertainment value they received. That was because of the novelty of the mike system, its loud broadcasts, and its beacon call to all around, that something unique in the realm of entertainment was taking place at the wedding house. Later, Indian orchestras replaced the mike men at these events, but the orchestras needed the microphones from the mike man for amplification of their singers' voices, so the mike man was once again part of the celebrations, but more in the background. In this way, even though the mike man was pushed into the background when the Indian orchestra provided entertainment for the cooking night audiences, he remained a necessary ingredient at the cooking nights. In addition, he played Indian film songs before the orchestra played music (usually 5 p.m. to 8 p.m.), during intervals, after the band completed its entertainment program (usually after 2 a.m. Sunday) and when the dulaha's

Ramash Ramsumair and a mike man pose for a photo at
Enchanted Garden Banquet Hall, Tableland.

bhaaraatians (boy's side entourage) took to the road to journey to the dulahin's home. In most of those rural communities, there was no electricity in the 1950s and early 1960s, so the mike operations were done with battery power.

Ramash Ramsumair an avid mike enthusiast, recalled as a young man, "attending several cooking nights in our area with my father and my siblings where the main entertainment was the music of the mike men. It was a very exciting time for us, and I must state I looked forward to going to those cooking nights as I loved to listen to the music of the mike men. One of the cooking nights that stand out for me took place several miles away from our home when one of my aunts was getting married. We lived at a place called Corosan in Tableland and the wedding was miles away at a place called Warwell Village. We walked several miles across villages, through forest tracts and lagoons and across the large Ortoire River on a makeshift bridge on our way to the cooking night/wedding house. It was a long distance to walk, but it was well worth it to listen to the music of the mike men. There was a very large crowd at the cooking night. Cooking nights in those days were very joyous occasions and we looked forward to attending them whether near or far from where we lived. There was no electricity in the area and so the mike man powered the mike system with batteries which were intermittently charged by a motorcar.

"The mike man stood out in the crowd and was like a star boy in his own right as everyone looked to him to play their favourite songs. People walked for hours to get to the venue and then sat or stood around in the tents and listened to the music of the mike man. Often when a popular song was played one could hear a loud chorus of approval from the audience. Sometimes individuals shouted across to the mike man to play a particular song and a few minutes later the mike man would play the requested song with a nod in the direction of the individual who had requested it. That was a big moment for the individual who had requested a song from the mike man as he felt a sense of self-importance with everyone looking towards him and those nearby congratulating him on his choice of song.

"Years later, as I entered the business world, I established the Simplex Complex as a venue to host events such as concerts, weddings and other entertainment events. A few years ago, the venue underwent a name change to Enchanted Garden Banquet Hall. Over the years we have hosted hundreds of Hindu weddings at the venue and most weddings had one thing in common, a well-decorated mike car leading the wedding entourage. The decorations on the mike car were usually in natural flowers or paper flowers but it was beautifully done.

"The mike car, which was usually the lead car in the wedding procession, played Indian film songs throughout the journey from the dulaha or dulahin's house to the Banquet Hall. It was like a call to action for villagers as people came out to the roadside to see and hear the mike as it passed their way. Even today youngsters still come out and stand by the wayside to see the mike as it passed."

Likewise, Ishmael Hoosaney, a mike man for 50 years, noted: "One of the stories that I remember is that some years ago in the 1970s, one of my cousins was getting married in Brothers Road, Rio Claro. There was no electricity in the area at the time, so I had to put together a system with five or six batteries for the occasion. At the time, I usually used two batteries; one was a backup, and that consistently carried me through the sessions from Saturday night to Sunday evening. However, in this case, I had to organize things in such a way because I had to play for the entire Saturday night and the Sunday on battery power only. In addition to that, I was commissioned to provide light in the kitchen for the roti makers during the Saturday night, and there was a challenge providing the light and keeping my mike system going. Nevertheless, the six batteries did the job; I mention this episode to indicate the various challenges that the mike man had to face to please his host and the audiences." [9]

Similarly, Krishna Timol, who grew up in the 1950s and 60s attending cooking night sessions with his uncles and other mike men, indicated: "Some of my best days of playing the mike system have been at the cooking nights. At first, we played the 78 RPM records, but then when the long play albums came out, we also started to use those and played all the songs from a particular movie at the time. We attracted lots of people, both male and female, who befriended us and made requests of us to play their favourite songs. We were very accommodating to them, especially female members of the audience or members of the host family who came to us with specific requests. It was a delightful time, especially when the young girls came and sat with us requesting specific songs, looking at the record jackets and the records being played. Sometimes they even helped us select some of the songs to play. It was an enjoyable time, and I met some of those young ladies after the cooking night at prearranged settings. Some of those remained friends for a long time after, and through those associations, I always got work, being called back to those areas and the opportunity to renew other acquaintances.

"The treatment I received as a mike man whenever I went into the villages to play at cooking nights was extraordinary. They treated me as one of their own. I was not a stranger there. When it came to food and drinks, the host ensured that I had no cause to complain about anything. The hosts always did their best to accommodate my wishes, and in turn, I made sure that they were pleased with my services because once they were satisfied, I knew that they would spread the word to other people around. Wherever I played, I always left a good name there, and because of that, I was frequently called back to work in those areas.

"On cooking nights on the girl's side, when I stopped playing the mike system at about 3 a.m. or 4 a.m., I usually helped the ladies to prepare talkarrie ingredients such as cleaning of pumpkin, mango and potato for cooking the next morning. The mike system usually stayed there for the entire weekend, and I stayed with it and with the host family for that time. I was welcomed and treated like a member of the family. I usually took a change of clothes with me, and I was allowed to shower and refresh myself at the home of my host. The people treated me well, and for years after my service to the family, our friendship remained intact, and whenever I passed that area, that friendship was always renewed."

Comparing playing at the cooking nights in the 1960s and today's world with DJ sound (box) systems, Timol further noted: "in those days the mike man was given special treatment and was elevated to the status of a kind of celebrity in the village. That was perhaps mainly because, in those days, very few people owned radios or television sets, so Indian film music was not as accessible as it is today, and for that reason, they looked forward to hearing the music of the mike men.

"That is unlike today where sometimes you go on a job, and no one cares, and the mike man or the DJ is not even offered water. Sometimes, he is not even offered a meal because the meals are catered for according to the number of people invited, and you have to be okay with it. In today's world, some people feel that because they are paying you to do a job, they need not provide you with any other services such as meals or drinks. However, that is today's world, and it goes with the territory nowadays. I do not make a fuss over it. But those early days were truly the glory days for the mike men.

"Today, almost every home has its own little music set up, and they can play music at their leisure. Depending on the extent of their investment in their music set up, they can play thunderous music and be content with it, but

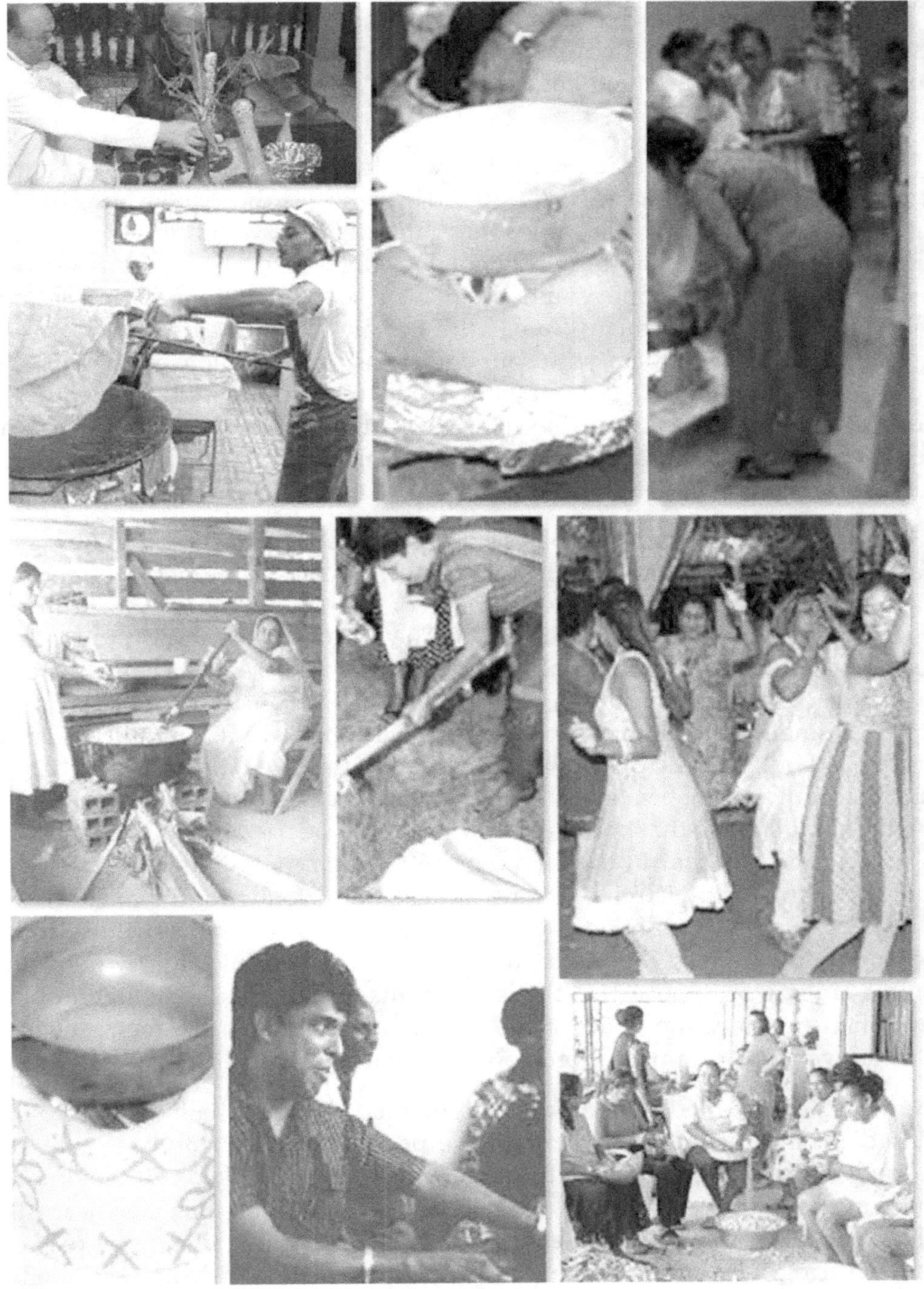

Scenes of the Cooking Night at the Hindu Wedding.

nothing beats the sound that comes out of the funnels of the mike system. When you compare the sound that comes out of the boxes on the DJ sound system with what is produced from the mike system, the music that emanates from the mike system is unique and has a special appeal.

"Everyone has his preference, and some people still prefer to listen to the music being played by the mike system rather than the boxes. I have heard complaints about too much bass with the boxes, but that is a complaint we never get with the mike system.

"I must also point out that in the early days of Indian orchestras in this country, it was the mike man that provided sound systems for these orchestras to play and sing. In those early days, most amplifiers only carried one microphone, and that microphone had to be switched around regularly. If you wanted to have a second microphone, you had to have a second amplifier working with the system. So, in those early days, the Indian orchestras depended on the mike man to provide them with sound systems. But as time went by, and the box systems came into being, they moved away from the mike system to the box systems mainly because those box systems had more microphones and connections for amplification of specific instruments in the orchestra. However, it is essential to note that they started with the mike man.

"Similarly, the mike men also played for religious occasions such as Ramayan Yaagnas or Bhagwat Yaagnas. In such cases, he had only one amplifier and one microphone. Usually, however, I always took with me an additional microphone with a long cord that would be set up for the pundit to read his sermon. The second microphone was usually set up on a stage some distance away for a religious group to sing bhajans. So, when the group on stage stopped singing rather than moving the microphone to the pundit, I simply just pulled out one microphone and plugged in the other one into the channel and manipulated the system quickly in that way. As time went by, I added another amplifier so that both microphones could be used simultaneously. But it was a time like that in the 1950s and 60s when microphones were scarce and expensive, and people welcomed the setting even with one microphone. However, those microphones were a lot different to the types we use today because, with singers, the microphones were so powerful that it would pick up the singing voice and also the instruments nearby. Thus, the microphone amplified not only the voice of the singer but also the instruments nearby. Nowadays, there's a microphone for every major instrument."

In the 1950s and 1960s, the mike man emerged without challenge as the key ingredient in the cooking night and the people from near and far gathered at the wedding house to listen to the ' music from the mike.' But playing the mike in the Hindu wedding eventually turned out to be a challenge for the mike man as it grew from just entertainment to the timely playing of relevant songs during the various Hindu wedding rituals. He learned to be skilled in his selection of appropriate songs according to the rituals performed during the wedding spanning from Friday night through Sunday evening.

Anand Boxer, Vice President of the Mike Men's Association who has been a mike man for over forty-five years indicated that during Hindu weddings, from the Hardi night through the cooking night and the wedding day, as a mike man he recalled playing his mike for as little as twenty dollars in the early days. He noted that in some cooking night sessions the Classical Singing went on into the Sunday morning.

As the years went by the visibility of the mike men at cooking nights diminished. Imtiaz Ali, who has been a mike man for over 25 years, lamented the demise of the mike men at the cooking nights and noted that "the cooking nights of the fifties and sixties, when a mike man played there, were the best days of the mike men. He emerged as the star attraction at the cooking nights playing Indian film songs and thus became a cultural icon for East Indians. I sometimes wish that we could see a return to those days when the mike man could go into the wedding tents and play for the entire session."[10]

While in the early years of their development in the country they were considered outcasts by some, by dint of their hard work and perseverance, the mike men created a cultural space for themselves at the cooking night, Sunday wedding entourage, and roaming through the countryside plying their trade. Equally, the East Indians' love for Indian film music was a positive reinforcement for them in creating a niche in the market. In time, they overcame all obstacles and emerged as torch bearers of Indian cultural in the country.

---

10   Imtiaz Ali. San Juan. Telephone interview. 02/01/20

32

A Mike man relaxes while playing his mike system

CHAPTER 3

Hindi Film Songs and the Mike Man

"I do not think anyone at the time really knew or understood the critical role that the mike men played in the development of Indian culture, Indian cinema, and Indian songs in this country." Ramesh Boodhoo.

The mike man's stock in trade was the Hindi film songs, and those songs came from Indian movies. The mike man made an exceptional effort to acquaint himself with the latest releases of Indian films and Indian film songs and sought to avail himself of the records, usually 78 RPM vinyl records, that were released with the Indian movies. Normally, the records–the film songs–arrived on the island years before the movie was released in the country.

Ramjattan Ramdeowar noted: "as a mike man I went to see almost every Indian film that was released in Trinidad so that I was very well aware of the songs and the movies, so if anyone asked me a question about a song or the movie I always had an answer available for them. It was a great pleasure indeed going to see the Indian movies first in the tent cinemas and then in the real cinemas. In those days, we paid six cents or twelve cents to go to the cinema, and I loved going to the cinema to see Indian movies.

"I got most of my records from Razack in San Juan. Some I bought; others were complementary to publicize the movie to be released in the coming months. But almost every cooking night when I played certain songs, there were always people who wanted to know what Indian movie that song was derived from, and so, in those early days, I used to make some minor announcements about new songs and the films to be released soon. I recall one time I mentioned a song and told the audience that the movie would be released in the next few months and I continued making such announcements as time went by. About a year later, at another cooking night, I played the song and made the announcement once more, and someone in the audience shouted, 'ah hearing you say that for more than a year now and the picture eh come yet.' But we had no control over the release of these Indian movies in Trinidad but as mike men, we did a great job in publicizing the songs before the films were released and by doing that when the films were released, they were big hits as many people went to see the movies because of the songs they heard us play from such pictures."

Ramesh Boodhoo, a cinema proprietor at Sangre Grande, further elaborated: "the mike men were a blessing to us, cinema owners. They came at a time when Indian movies were just picking up in the country a few years after the release of that first Indian movie in Trinidad–Bala Joban. I do not think anyone at the time really knew or understood the critical role that the mike men played in the development of Indian culture, Indian cinema, and Indian songs in this country. I think that had it not been for the mike men of the 1950s and 60s, Indian culture in this country would have been at a low ebb. While we depended on the mike men to publicize the Indian movies and Indian songs, they played a tremendous role in the evolution of Indian culture in this country. I do not think people in the rural areas would have known, or would have been exposed to so many Indian songs if the mike man did not go into those areas and play songs at cooking nights and advertise the movies for us. We paid the mike men to journey through the villages to popularize the Indian movies just before they were to be shown at the cinema. As they drove through the rural areas, they played songs from the movies and made announcements about the showing of the movie. I know of some mike men who just drove through the villages playing Indian songs just for the fun of it, and it was these mike men who became stars in their own right in these villages and surrounding areas. People just loved to listen to the beautiful music that came out from the funnels of the mike system as the mike men traversed the countryside.

"Many people loved to hear the echo of the loud sounds as the mike man continued their journey through the villages. I can tell you that some of these 'mikes' were heard for miles around, and people stood by on the side of the road long after the mike man had gone his way. They played a tremendous role in publicizing Indian film songs, and it was because of their input in the development of Indian film songs in this country that when Indian orchestras came on the scene, people were able to appreciate the songs and music of the Indian orchestras because they too also played mainly Indian film songs. I have been to cooking nights where Indian orchestras provided entertainment for the night, and when they played Indian film songs, they had the full attention of the audience. However, when the orchestras introduced a local Indian classical song or a folk song, they lost the attention of a great part of the audience since many people felt that those songs were long and boring and they only wanted to listen to the very catchy, melodious film songs."[11]

Similarly, Deoraj Harrikissoon, 94, a retired cane worker, recalling the heydays of the mike men of the 1950s and 60s, stated: "the mike man was an integral part of Indian culture in this country and it is because of their hard work that Indian culture in this country was kept alive. They traveled to every nook and cranny of this country to ply their trade, and sometimes they did it even for free or for half price depending on the customer. In those days, there was no electricity in most of the rural areas where Indians lived, but the mike man with his battery-operated system went into the villages, traces, bushy areas, cane estates, and other areas bringing light and life to those sleepy areas. If it

11   Ramesh Boodhoo., Personal Interview, Sangre Grande. 15/05/08

were not for the mike men, those areas would never have been exposed to such aspects of Indian culture. They are the ones who kept Indian culture alive in the villages and cane areas. We have to be thankful to those courageous sons of the indentured workers who braved all kinds of weather to get to places where they were hired to play.

" I remember the time when a mike man had to play at a wedding at one of my relatives who lived at the deep end of a side trace in Manahambre. We had to push the mike car through the muddy road for almost a quarter-mile to get to the wedding house and all the way the mike played beautiful songs to encourage us to push the car through the mud. I was young at the time, and it was fun, but when I look back now, I realize that that era has passed on and very few mike men, if any, would venture into such areas today." [12]

On the other hand, Dipchand Maharaj, a former school supervisor and cultural aficionado, observed: "the era of the mike man when he was in his heyday is gone never to return. They came at a time when East Indians in this country needed a cultural push, and they provided that push by venturing into the countryside where the Indians resided. They were loved and adored and were akin to movie stars wherever they went to ply their trade in this country. Growing up in my village in Cunaripo, I can recall many of us youngsters running behind the mike car as it drove through the community blasting away the Indian film songs that were popular at the time. Every one of us loved to listen to the Indian film songs, and so when the mike came into the area, we could hear it from a mile away, and we came out to the roadside to see the mike. It was a huge thing in those days when the mike man came to the area because not very often did they rove in those areas. The mike man was a symbol of Indian culture in this country and still is, even though he is seen less and less at Indian cultural events and more and more in announcing for stores and political parties.

"Every mike man was very knowledgeable about Indian movies and the songs that came from those movies. It was the playing of songs from Indian films that made the mike men so popular among the East Indians because they fell hook, line and sinker for those catchy songs. I recall there was a mike man who lived in the village, and every so often, especially on weekends when he was not employed elsewhere, he would put on his mike system and play those beautiful film song melodies for the entire village to enjoy. We stayed in our homes and listened to those beautiful songs and looked forward to hearing him play the Indian songs on a Sunday morning and on evenings during the week. Many people learned several of the Indian film songs by just listening to him play those songs every week. Even after he had stopped playing his music for the day, people were heard humming the songs as they went about their chores.

---

[12]　　Doeraj Harrikissoon. Personal Interview, Princes Town. 22/03/10

"There was a young man in my village who sang with an orchestra, and he often went to the home of the mike man to have him play his favourite songs repeatedly while he copied the words as best he could. For us, the playing of the mike was never a nuisance, or never too loud. We all loved to hear the loud music. You know I must tell you that with Indian songs, Indian film songs, there are several songs you can only enjoy if it is played loudly on the mike system through the funnel and the mike men knew those songs well and played them as loudly as they could, and we all enjoyed them. But make no mistake about this, while the mike man is probably on the way out, I am of the considered view that he would still be here 50 years from now plying his trade and keeping the Indian film songs alive, especially what we call the oldie film songs."[13]

Commenting on the work of the mike men, James Ramnath, a former Presbyterian school principal of Sangre Grande, summed it up well when he said: "whether you were Hindu, Muslim, Christian or other religious faith, most Indians loved Indian music. In those early days of the mike man, there were very few Indian programs on the radio, so we depended heavily on the work of the mike man, and he brought the Indian songs closer to us at weddings, at Ramayanas and other social events such as bazaars. At bazaars at our Presbyterian schools, the mike man played Indian songs most of the time, and everyone enjoyed those songs. When there was a wedding in the village, everyone went there to listen to the songs played by the mike man. And in those days, you did not have to be invited to a wedding to attend a cooking night. Once we heard that there was a cooking night in the village, or a community nearby, we went to listen to the Indian songs played on the mike.

"The songs the mike men played were all film songs from Indian movies, most of which we had not seen because for us it was very costly to go to the cinema to see an Indian movie, but we loved the songs and those songs were brought into our communities, into our villages, into our homes by the mike man and we owe them a debt of gratitude for making those Indian film songs so accessible to us. As I understand it, those mike men were ever busy adding Indian film songs to their repertoire. And they only played a type of record called the 78 RPM vinyl records. 78 RPM meant that the record spins 78 times per minute on the turntable. Those 78 RPM records are no longer manufactured, and so the mike men of today have a huge task of getting those types of records from people who kept them as souvenirs."[14]

Despite the scarcity of the 78 RPM records the mike men continued to make an important contribution to the cultural fabric of the nation as Sonia Maharaj, 85, of Rio Claro observed: "the mike man came from a special breed of people. He took his job very seriously and went all out to make it a success and to please his audience. He made every effort to collect records from people near and far, sometimes paying a considerable sum for the record because he wanted it so badly. Every mike man tried to have a copy of the most popular songs,

---

13   Dipchand Maharaj. Personal Interview. St. Augustine. 29/01/10
14   James Ramnath. Personal Interview, Sangre Grande. 20/08/08

especially of the oldie songs people loved so much. He spent almost every waking moment trying to improve his collection and his mike system. You wanted to know about the religious songs that the mike man played?

"The mike man played religious songs at religious events like Ramayan and Bhagwat Yaagnas. They played bhajans from movies such as Baiju Bawra, Tulsidas, Bhagwat Mahima, and others. I remember that in the 1950s, Bhagwat Yaagnas were very popular, and at every yaagna, the song *Bhagwat Bhagwan ki hai aarti* (Bhagwat Mahima) was sung at the beginning and end of the prayer session. Every mike man wanted to have a copy of that song and played it before and after the reading by the pundit. There were other religious film songs that people loved to hear, and the mike man always made it his duty to please the people, so sometimes he borrowed songs from friends–other mike men–to play them at the yaagnas."

Reflecting on the song *Bhagwat Bhagwan ki hai aarti* that Sonia Maharaj mentioned above, Ramdeowar, in a previous interview insisted it was because of the mike men that the pundits became aware of that song as they regularly played it at the yaagnas before and after each session. Ramdeowar recalled that once, at a Bhagwat, where he was the mike man, the officiating pundit was not feeling well. When it was time for the aarti song at the beginning of the session, he was asked to play the *Bhagwat Bhagwan ki hai aarti* record. At the end of the night's session, he was again asked to play the same song, and the people were invited to sing along with it. Everyone liked it and for the rest of the yaagna, that was the modus operandi for the aarti.

While that might well be how it all started, in time, that particular song became the most popular aarti bhajan sung at Bhagwat Yaagnas in Trinidad. It is still popular today and is sung at Bhagwats regularly. According to Ramdeowar, it was the work of the mike men that popularized that song in the country and at Bhagwat Yaagnas and helped to make it an aarti song. From research conducted by this writer, Trinidad is the only country in the Indian Diaspora where a filmi song was taken and made a part of the religious rituals of the Hindu Religion as was done with *Bhagwat Bhagwan ki hai aarti* and Bhagwat Yaagnas.[15]

Sonia Maharaj continued: "Another thing I remember about the mike man and the yaagnas was that to make up the time, he often played non-religious popular songs, but no one complained because that was acceptable at the time. Today, the pundits demand that they play only religious songs at the yaagnas. Every year at the kutiya in my village, we organized a Panchoutie Ramayan Yaagna and Bhagwat Yaagna, and a mike man from the neighboring village came to supply the mike system. For the Ramayan Yaagna, I remember he used to arrive early at about 4 p.m. and play songs before the pooja started at 6 o'clock. Many people came early just to listen to the mike man play those songs. We sometimes joked that the mike man was interrupted by the pundit's

---

15   Gooptar, 2012.cpp210-211.

discourse as he continued to play music after the yaagna had ended for the night. He sometimes played for an hour after the yaagna and most people stayed back to listen to the mike songs.

"In those days, there was no feeding after the Ramayan was over, so it was not like he was playing music while people were eating. In those days, you received Parsaad in your hand, on a small piece of paper at the end of the yaagna, and that was the end of proceedings for the night. But the mike man continued playing his music, and we all remained just to hear him play the Indian film songs. I do not think he was paid for playing that extra set of music. He just did it out of love, out of pleasure, and it pleased us all to hear such lovely songs. It was at that time that he played a lot of his non-religious film songs that we were accustomed to because by that time, the pundit had already left. We just sat back and listened to the songs. And in those days in yaagnas in the village, we did not have chairs to sit on; we sat on benches and palls or dried fig straw on the ground. But I will tell you this; with all the improvements in music today with the big-box and all those new fancy public address systems, if I had to do it all over, I would never give up the mike man of the 1950s and 60s. Those were glorious and memorable days." [16]

Indeed, for many people those were the most glorious days of the mike men as Dipchand Maharaj affirmed: "the mike men were part of us, and we were part of them. In a sense, we made them into folk heroes, and they, in turn, gave us a great tradition and inheritance. Those mike men took the songs from India and brought it to us in the villages and into our homes long before the radio did so. I must tell you that in those days we did not have radios in the villages as they do today. A few people in the rural communities owned radios, and many of us went to those homes to listen to the Indian songs on the radio station when the Indian program was aired on Friday evenings. But it was the mike men who came to the village regularly, just driving through playing Indian songs that brought music and joy into our lives."

In consonance with similar views expressed elsewhere by others in this book, Sonia Maharaj added a personal nostalgic touch when she said: "it was such a joy to go to a cooking night in those days and listen to the mike man blast out those Indian songs. People used to get up and dance when certain songs were played, and so the mike men knew to play those songs a few times before the night was over, and each time, people would get up and dance. It was fun to see them enjoy themselves while most of us just loved to sit and listen to the music.

"Indian weddings in those days lasted three days, and the mike man always came early on a Saturday evening and left late on a Sunday evening. He played almost the entire night–on Saturday night– probably took an hour's sleep in the morning and then by 9 a.m. next morning was playing his music and this

---

went on for the rest of the day except for that time when the pundit performed the marriage ceremony and had to use the microphone. I still remember those days as some of the most glorious days of Indian songs and Indian culture in this country.

" The mike men were everywhere in the countryside where the Indians lived, and they were very popular among the people, and we loved them, cherished them, and made them feel welcomed and important. I do not know anyone in my village and surrounding areas who did not like listing to the music from the mike. As I said, the mike man was one of the most essential elements of the Hindu wedding setup. I had ten children, and eight got married under bamboo, and for all of them, I took (hired) mike men to play music for their weddings. I had six girls, and I could never forget the experience at the end of the wedding ceremony when those girls were leaving my house, and the mike man played songs like *Janay waley dulahin (Bete Bete)* and other similar songs that brought a sorrowful feeling inside me as my daughter was leaving my home. Even today, when I remember those moments, I can still hear the mike playing those songs, and I sit and sometimes cry because of the emotions that come up inside me.

" Sometimes when I hear those songs on the radio, those feelings come back to me - of the mike man playing the songs as my daughter left - and it still brings feelings of sadness to me. That was the power of the mike man in those days. If the mike man did not play those songs at that time, those memories would have been lost. Every time I hear those songs, I think of my daughters leaving my house and the mike playing those songs in the background."

Pickrani Gooptar, who was married in 1964 in Hindu rites, also reminisced about some nostalgic moments regarding her wedding day when she remarked: "an Indian wedding in the village was a big thing for the villagers and those in surrounding areas. When I got married in 1964, my father employed a mike man for the cooking night, and that was a huge thing in the village because, at that time, it was very rare to have a mike in such communities as the one where I lived (Plum Road). Even those who were not invited to the cooking night came out in their numbers to listen to the songs played by the mike man. Most of them, however, tended to remain at the roadside, but I recall my father going out to them and inviting them to come into the tent. My father was that kind of man, and whether the people were invited or not to the wedding, he welcomed them and made them feel comfortable. Most people spent the entire night listening to the mike man play his songs because that is not something that they were accustomed to, and they just loved to listen to the Indian songs.

"On the Sunday of the wedding when the baaraat (entourage from the dulaha's side) arrived at my home there was a clash—a friendly competition—between the two mike systems and the people enjoyed the friendly encounter as they played some of the most beautiful and popular Indian songs.

"On the way back to my husband's home after the wedding, the mike led the entourage and played Indian film songs nonstop. One song he played several times on the journey was 'Ye To Kaho, Kaun Ho Tum…. Yes my darling' (who are you) from the movie Akeli Mat Jaiyo, [Don't go alone] (1963). It was one of the popular songs at the time and very appropriate for the occasion. That song still lingers in my memory even today, and it brings back nostalgic reminiscences of my wedding day. Every time I hear that song, I remember my wedding day and the mike man playing that beautiful song."[17]

Discussing the popularity of the mike men in the 50s and 60s, Ranjit Singh, 94, (Penal), an accomplished mike man of the Golden Era of Indian cinema, remarked: "in my days the mike was very popular, and everyone wanted to hear us play at weddings, parties and school bazaars. I enjoyed playing the mike everywhere, but two of the most memorable times for me were the cooking nights and when I drove through the village playing the mike. On Saturdays and Sundays, when I did not have a job, that is, a job to play at somebody's home, I used to pick up one or two friends and drive slowly through several villages nearby playing some of the top-rated Indian songs on the mike. Wherever we went, there were always people coming out to look at us (to look at the mike) and I had a pair of the big long funnel mikes. That was really a thing of beauty. I painted it in a bright blue with the name 'Sonny Boy' written on it because Sonny Boy was my home name, so when I bought my mike, I naturally put that name on it, and everyone came to know me by that name.

" In addition to the men, women and children and even the elderly who came out and lined the roadside to hail us and ask us to play a song for them, were the men who came out of the bars to greet us and often offered us a beer. These were men we never knew, but they waved us down, offered us a beer, chatted with us for a few minutes before we continued on our journey. I remember on a few occasions we actually came out of the car and went into the bar to have a beer with some of the guys, and one of my men remained in the car and continued playing the mike. When we came out from the bar, there was always a huge crowd gathered around the mike just curious, just looking on or listening to the mike. I think for a lot of people, just being close to those enormous funnels was some kind of achievement. Some youngsters even wanted to touch them."[18]

Siew Lalchan (Cedros), 88, who had been a mike man for over 35 years, added an interesting angle to the life of a mike man that concerned the mike man and his encounters with the opposite sex. He stated: "… another exciting thing for me in my youthful days was to observe the beautiful young girls who came out to look at the mike and to greet us. I was young and a bachelor at the time, and several of the young girls attracted my attention, and I would go back into those villages driving slowly, hoping that the beautiful girls I had seen before

---

17   Pickrani Gooptar. Personal Interview. San Rafael, Arima. 8/11/19
18   Ranjit Singh, 94, Penal. Former mike man. Telephone interview,15/3/17.

would come out and wave at me. Sometimes I saw them; sometimes, they were not there. Then, one particular Sunday morning in 1965, I was driving through one of the nearby villages when I spotted this extremely beautiful young lady who came out with her family and stood on the side of the road waving to me as I passed. I slowed down, and her father asked me to play a song from Mother India, and I said, 'okay.' Then I asked the young lady if she would like me to play a song for her, and she told me to play any song that I thought she would like. I played the song *Jawan hai Mohabbat* by Noor Jahan from the movie *Anmol Ghadi* for her and told her 'this is your song.' Then I played the song from *Mother India* for her father as I drove off.

"On my return, as I neared her home once more, I played the song again for her, and she was there again by the roadside. I slowed down and asked her if she liked the song, and she said it was the best Indian song she ever heard. After that, every time I went into that area, I played that song for her. It was like I was calling out to her and every time she came out to the roadside to greet me. It was like that song was creating a bond between us, something I did not even realize at the time.

"Then one Sunday morning when I passed, she was there standing alone at the roadside. I stopped and chatted with her, and a relationship began to develop. Her name was Shanti. A few months later my mother asked me 'if after driving my mike around the whole country, I had not picked up a daughter-in-law for her as yet?' and after some prodding, I told her about the beautiful young lady I had seen and if I had to marry anyone it would be that young lady. For weeks after that, my mother kept insisting she wanted to know where the young lady lived. So one Sunday morning I took her with me in the car when I went playing the mike along the road and as we reached the house I stopped and again the young lady came out with her parents. We chatted for a few minutes, and I played that song again for her and then we left.

"Unknown to me, a few days later, my mother hired a taxi and went to Shanti's home. She had gone to them with a proposal for marriage, and Shanti's parents immediately accepted, knowing that they had seen me so often in the area, but they said that they had never known that I was interested in their daughter. They indicated to her that it would be up to Shanti to give the final word, which she did without hesitation. I told my mother I was always afraid to talk to Shanti about anything else because her parents were always there with her, but I think that she knew that I liked her and I sensed that she had some feelings for me. So, when my mother told me she had been to Shanti's home to arrange my marriage, I was speechless, I could not say a word. I was astonished. It was a shock to me. I went and I touched my huge blue mike funnels and said, 'thank you; you not only brought me happiness with music, but you brought me a wife.' We were married soon after, and we had eight lovely children, all girls.

"None of my sons-in-law or grandchildren were interested in continuing with the mike business, so a few years ago, we sold the hundreds of 78 vinyl records I kept over the years. It was there just lying about and not being used. A friend from the north was looking for those types of 78 RPM records, and he heard that I had a lot of them, and he came and offered me a price, and I accepted it, and he took the records off my hand. I told my wife those records reminded me of her; it was because of those records that I found her, and that is why I did not want to get rid of them. A few years later, she passed away. But I have no regrets about my life as a mike man, and I hope that there will always be young men willing to step forward and carry on the traditions of the mike man."[19]

Another mike man, Johnny M., who wished to remain anonymous, told a personal story about his mother and the mike system. He explained: "I was about 24 years old working at a factory in San Fernando. I lost my job and found it difficult to find another job. For almost eight months, I roamed everywhere looking for a job but could not find anything to my liking. Then one day, one of my uncles visited, and I heard my mother telling him about my predicament and that I could not find a job. He was getting old, and he had a beautiful mike system which he called 'Jatayu.' He had stopped playing the mike for a few years because of illness and suggested to my mother that if I were interested, he would teach me what I needed to know about the mike system, and I could earn a living by playing mike at weddings and other events.

"At first, my mother was not so happy with the proposal, but then she called me and, in his presence, mentioned it to me. I grabbed the opportunity and thus began my career as a mike man. I did not have any money to pay my uncle for the system, but my mother promised him that she would pay for it over some time. I never knew whether she paid him or not, but I worked and saved money and offered her the money to pay my uncle for the system, and she told me, 'do not worry, I already paid your uncle.' Later, after her passing, I learned that her brother had borrowed some money from her some years earlier, and although she never asked him for it, he considered giving me the mike system payment for the loan. I played that system everywhere, and I came to love it, and it became part of me, part of my life, and part of my family. I eventually found a job and continued to play the mike system on weekends and during weekdays when I announced for the cinemas.

"Some of the most memorable times for me playing the mike was at the wedding on a Sunday, when the dulaha's side mike met up with the dulahin's side mike, and we had friendly mike battles. And the battle went like this. The other mike would play a song that was very popular and well-loved by the people. After that song, I would play a song I thought would be more popular than the one he played. And for the entire evening, we would alternate like this and the winner would usually be the one with more people dancing and singing when he played his songs. We gauged our popularity by how people reacted to the songs we played. If I played a song and I saw no reaction from the people, I would know to change the type of song the next time to get some response from the people. We chose our songs and played to audiences based on their responses.

---

19   Siew Lalchan, 94, Cedros. Telephone interview. 2/9/17

"Sometimes in a cooking night, we would be looking at the people as we played a song to gauge if we should play that song again. From the responses of the audience, we also understood if to continue to play that type of song. It was difficult for us to go into an area, especially a new area, and not know what kind of music the people loved, so it was essential for us to be on the lookout and to gauge what kind of songs the people liked as we played on. Sometimes the people will tell us 'change that song' or 'that is a boss song,' and so we knew if to continue along that line or not. They also made requests which served to guide us along that journey. The most popular and most requested songs were those by Mohammed Rafi and duets involving him. I played songs by other Indian singers, but wherever I went, most people preferred to listen to songs by Mohammed Rafi.

"When my uncle passed away, I went to play at his funeral, and that is where I met my future wife. She was from the same village, and she was there helping the family, and I noticed her and smiled at her. She smiled back at me and left me to my own devices. I continued to play some popular bhajans as I thought those songs would be fitting for a funeral. Then, sometime later, she came and asked me to play some 'appropriate sad funeral songs.' I listened to her and then looked through my stack of records to choose the kind of songs she requested. A little later, when she passed my way, I asked her if those were the songs she wanted to hear, and she told me with a big, bright smile, 'yes, you are doing great.'

"I had played at several funerals before, but it was the first time that anyone had criticized me, asking me to play some sad music at a funeral. After the funeral, I made it my duty to speak with her and to thank her for her input, and that began a long and enduring relationship. We were married nine months later. So, my uncle gave me the mike, and in his parting–at this funeral, I met my wife. Ironic indeed."

Regarding the important role of the mike men in the community, Mulchan Singh, 74, a farmer of Princes Town, spoke in glowing terms about the mike men and the vital role they played in bringing Indian music to the country areas. However he also indicated that there were one or two mike men in the old days who brought into disrepute the great work of the mike men. He mentioned two incidents he witnessed involving mike men, one in Princes Town and the other in Rio Claro: "In the Princes Town incident, a popular mike man from Chaguanas came to perform his services at a cooking night at the home of one of his relatives. He had donated his services free since he did not wish to put the burden of finance on his relations. A mike man from the area who had heard about a wedding a few months before and had approached the bride's father for the job was angry when his offer was rejected. On the cooking night when the mike man from Chaguanas was playing in the wedding tent, bottles and stones rained on the tent for over five minutes, and everyone scampered away, leaving the mike man and his system in the tent. No one was hurt, but it was a common belief in the village that the mike man who was rejected for the job was responsible for the havoc that night. After half an hour, the music continued, and there was no further disturbance during the night.

"A similar incident occurred a few villages away when a mike man from outside the district was once again brought in to play at a cooking night. This time the mike man from the area and a few of his goons went to the cooking night and heckled the mike man telling him repeatedly that he was playing 'crap,' 'stupidness,' and 'boring' songs. The situation came to a head when the owner of the house, the host, approach them and asked them to leave, telling them that they were not invited to the cooking night. At first, they resisted, but a relative of the host, who was a policeman intervened, showed them his badge, and demanded that they either leave or behave themselves. They went out to the roadside and remain there for the rest of the night, and no one took them on.

"In the other incident at Rio Claro during the Sunday wedding, when the two mike men clashed, (one from the dulaha's side and the other from the dulahin's side) they staged a 'Battle of the Mikes,' and people seemed to be enjoying the session. There were two groups of men, one set by each mike system supporting their mike man. As the battle of songs continued, the two groups of men drew closer together as the minutes went by and soon, they were facing each other. As the mike men played their songs, at first alternating; then they played songs simultaneously trying to drown out each other's mike system. Things came to a head, and supporters of the two mike men clashed.

"So, while the wedding ceremonies were taking place inside the tent, some distance away, supporters of the two mike men were performing a different set of rituals outside, fighting each other. The two mike men tried to stop the fracas, but the one from the dulaha's side got a busted nose. People from both sides parted the fight and asked the mike men to stop playing for the evening. After about an hour, one of the mike men, the one from the dulahin's side, played his mike with no further incidents for the evening. Later, when the other mike man left with the baaraat, the mike man from the dulahin's house played one of the most hilarious laughing songs from Indian films, as if laughing away the whole incident and laughing at the other mike man who got his nose busted.

"Those were isolated incidents. Generally, however, I discovered the mike men were usually amiable and got on well with each other, but as often happens in every setting, there are always one or two bad apples in the barrel that cause problems when you least expect them." [20]

Stocks, Stars and Style

The mike man as an entertainer was unique in the field of entertainment in Trinidad because he serviced a niche market that depended almost totally on imports (78 RPM Vinyl records) from India. This link with India and Indian film songs endeared him to his audiences, and soon he became a star in his

---

20   Mulchan Singh, Princes Town. Telephone interview.22/11/2019

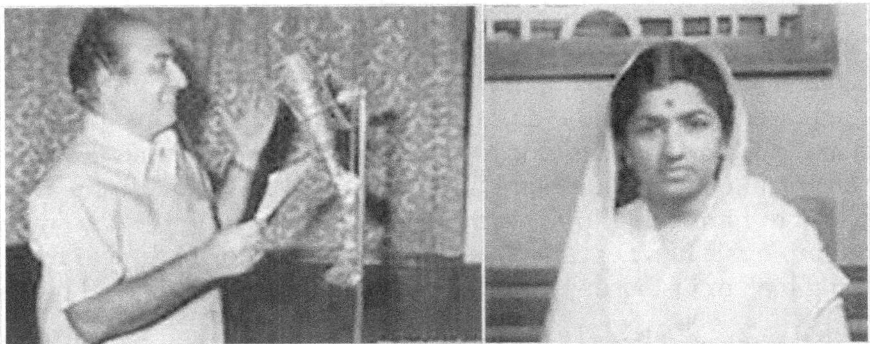

Mohammed Rafi and Lata Mangeshkar were the favourite playback singers of the mike men and the audiences alike.

own right as Kissoon noted: "the mike men played mainly in rural East Indian settlement areas of the country. His stock in trade was Indian film songs played from 78 RPM vinyl records imported from India," while Ramdeowar mentioned, "the mike man usually had a sizeable collection of records, literally running into the hundreds, which he took to the cooking night and other functions."

Hublal Ramkissoon, a mike man for many years, further indicated that their favourite Hindi film playback singers were Mohammed Rafi, Lata Mangeshkar, Hemant Kumar, Mukesh, Asha Bhosle, Mahendra Kapoor, Manna Dey and Talat Mahmood in that order.[21]

At the wedding house (as with other locations where he played), particularly at the cooking night, the mike man was the center of attraction. The celebrity status accorded the mike men created a stir among some audience members at cooking nights, and several people felt compelled to become acquainted with them.

Partap Sitahal, a mike enthusiast and avid cooking night follower of the 60s and 70s remarked: "There was a certain aura about the mike and the mike man, which caught the attention of audiences. Just to 'see' the mike passing was a great achievement for many. To be waved at or talked to by the mike man as he passed, was an honour for the average villager as they ran out of their homes to the roadside when they heard the mike in the distance. He held a unique, elevated position in the eyes of the villagers and the audience. From the moment he entered the village on Saturday evening playing his mike, to the time he left on Sunday evening, he enjoyed celebrity status among the villagers...".

Ramdeowar, a mike man for over 60 years, confirming Sitahal's assertion added: "women ran out with flour (dough) in their hands, as they lined the roadside to see the mike. People waved to us and made us feel special as we passed through the villages. Wherever the mike man played in those days, he was the center of attention, like a kind of star boy himself. People treated us special. People begged us to play their favourite songs, but we could only please a

<hr>

21   Hublal Ramkissoon. Personal Interview, Rio Claro.22/03/12

few. Playing the mike was the love of my life, and wherever I went, the people made me feel special…" while Baliram Ramoutar, a mike man for 50 years, also stated that he (the mike man), "was the man of the moment at cooking nights and weddings and the hosts and those around him instantly fulfilled his wishes." [22] Sitahal further indicated that "while many people wanted to get close to the mike man, to befriend him, to talk to him, to request a song; just being close to him, being in his company was adequate for the average East Indian filmi music fan. For others, just getting an acknowledgment from him, a knowing look or just a simple nod of the head meant a great deal to them."

Sitahal also suggested it was a major talking point to tell their friends that they knew the mike man, spoke to him or requested a song which he played. When a requested song was played, the person requesting the song often hailed out the mike man with a 'thank you mike man' or 'that is my song, I asked for that song,' so everyone present knew that he had requested that song. Sitahal recalled spending entire nights sitting next to mike men, chatting with them, and making special requests for songs not only on his behalf but also on behalf of other friends who channeled their requests to the mike man through him. This was a remarkable achievement for him as he (Sitahal) shared the center of attention, sitting next to the mike man. Everyone who had an encounter with the mike men felt a sense of importance and this added to the evolving image of the mike man as an Indian cultural icon among the people. In this way, the mike men gained in prominence, and many of them sought to create innovations on how they performed their duties.

78 RPM Vinyl Records

The mike man has traditionally used and continues to use the 78 RPM vinyl records to provide music that reverberates through the mike system, bringing

78 RPM Vinyl Records were the constant companions of the local mike men.

22   Baliram Ramoutar, Personal Interview, Couva. 22/8/10

78 RPM vinyl records used by the mike men of Trinidad.

joy and happiness to thousands of people throughout the country. Those records were produced in India to promote Indian movies. One of the unwritten formulas for Indian films was that each movie should have at least 5 to 8 songs.

Actors and actresses lip-synched those songs on screen recorded by playback singers such as Mohammed Rafi, Lata Mangeshkar, Mahendra Kapoor, Asha Bhosle, and others.

In the early days of Indian movies, only silent movies were produced, and it was not until 1931 with the production of the film Alam Ara that sound came to the Indian silver screen. In those early movies, the songs were recorded live on sets, and there were no playback singers because to be an actor or actress, one had to be able to sing in addition to their acting ability, so the actors sang their own songs for the movies. A few years later, playback singing was introduced in which case the actors no longer needed to sing their own songs, but they lip-synced the songs produced by other singers who became known as playback singers.

Whenever a movie was made in India, 78 RPM vinyl records were created as part of the overall production, and those records were sold both in India and in overseas diaspora countries such as Fiji, Mauritius, South Africa, Guyana, Surinam and Trinidad and Tobago. The mike men in Trinidad made optimum use of these 78 RPM Vinyl records which became his stock in trade. By the 1980s, with the revolution in the recording industry incorporating cassette tapes followed by CDs and DVDs, the production of the 78 RPM vinyl records became a thing of the past.

Randy Kissoon, speaking about the 78 RPM vinyl records revealed: "the mike men remain very nostalgic and generally play the oldies songs going back to the 1950s and 60s, even the 70s and sometimes the 80s, but the songs that are most popular with the mike men are those songs going back to the Golden Era of Indian movies–the 1950s and 1960s. In those days, when the Indian film industry released songs in Bombay, they were published on 78 RPM Vinyl records.

These vinyl records were originally produced in India. Production of those records ended years ago. They are very scarce to come by. The true mike man still uses these records, although he can easily use some of the digital systems available. The mike men and the listeners alike, believe that the sound that comes out from the 78 RPM records is unique, and so the mike men prefer to play the

Turntable or record player showing arm with cartridge at end of arm.

original soundtrack recordings from the 78 RPM vinyl records. Mike men in Trinidad and Tobago, who had amassed collections of these records, saw those records as rare gems and held on to them as collectors' items."

Darren Basdeo, a mike man for several years, referring to the rarity of the 78 RPM records stated: "the type of 78 RPM records that I have are no longer made in India and are considered to be very rare. As such, we consider them precious gems, and we do not lend as freely as we did in the early days.

"They have become collectors' items. A 78 RPM vinyl record, if it could be found, may cost a mike man $1000-$1500 to get it from India or on the Internet. It may be possible to get a few locally from private people who owned those records in the 1960s, but it is a challenging task since people who own those records tend to hold on to them. The mike men who own those records would not part with them for any amount of money.

"Most mike men have a relatively large collection of those songs amassed over the last 25 to 30 years, and often, it is an inheritance handed down from an older mike man to his son or nephew. My elder brother Deo Basdeo is also a mike man, and between us, we have an excellent collection of Indian film songs.

"Because those records are so rare, mike men take special care of those records and play them with due care and attention, so the records are not scratched. A lot depends on the kind of cartridge and needle used in the record player to determine whether the record gets scratched or not. The wrong type of needle or the wrong cartridge can create havoc for the record. When a record is scratched, the sound is distorted, and people do not like to hear such recordings. The cartridge refers to that part of the turntable arm at the end where the needle is inserted. Even needles for the record player are difficult to come by in Trinidad as there is no local supplier, so these have to be imported. However, fortunately for many of us mike men, most of the older generation of mike men bought large stocks of those needles, and so we inherited those stocks, and they are continuously being used. In my case, my uncles had hundreds of such needles, and so we received that stock. One needle can give us about three or four years of playing time."[23]

Randy Kissoon continuing the discussion about the 78 RPM vinyl records argued: "in the early days those records were relatively cheap, costing sometimes $0.25-$0.50 going up to a few dollars. Most mike men availed themselves of those records and built an excellent collection that was passed on to their children or others as needed. Today, it is very difficult to get these vinyl records. There are still some places in India and on the Internet where they are available. Depending on the era and the type of song, the price of a 78 RPM vinyl record can range from $1000 the $2500. And that is just for one record. Some mike men can have a collection of 200 to 300 of these records and sometimes more than that amount, so that tells you about the total value of the mike system. So, while on the one hand, you have the mike system itself, the mike men cannot operate without these records, so the records form an integral part of any mike system. It might well be said that because those records are

---

23   Darren Basdeo. Telephone interview.15/1019

rare and very expensive, the mike man mike might well be sitting on a precious asset valued at over \$200,000 to \$300,000. But no mike man worth his salt will sell those records unless he is going out of business.

"Another thing about those records, while a mike man might have 100 or 200 vinyl records, just a fraction of those are used regularly in the mike competitions. Perhaps only 25 or 30 may be useful for competition purposes, but the rest is generally used for weddings and entertainment purposes."

The 78 RPM vinyl records while popular with the mike men had its limitations in that its playing time was limited to around three minutes but several Bollywood film songs were longer than what could be accommodated on the 78 RPM records. As a result, one or two verses of the filmi songs were omitted from the recordings. Those verses were either removed from the middle or the end of songs such as *Sau Saal Pehle* (I have loved you a hundred years) from the movie *Jab Pyar Kisi Se Hota Hai* [1961] (when you fall in love), *Dil Loot Ne Wale* from *Madari* [1959] (Juggler). Many Hindi cinema fans had heard those songs many times during the previous year or two before the movie was released and some had even learnt the songs. They were pleasantly surprised at the added bonus of an extra verse or two of their favourite songs in the movie when they went to see the picture as these verses were never recorded on the 78 records. Some even returned to see the movie just to hear the new verse(s) of the songs. Today, however, with the availability of the internet and YouTube, at their convenience, they are able to easily access those video songs with the extra verses.

Record Players or Turntables

Another aspect of the mike man's ensemble is the turn table or record player that can play the 78 RPM vinyl records. Speaking about the record players, Basdeo further added, "there are some brands on the market such as Numark, Ion, Seco, Rivera, and Sharp that some of the mike men still use. The Seco, Rivera and Sharp brands are the older ones and are very difficult to come by. The Numark brand, however, is relatively new and is manufactured in such a way that the record players can play the 78 RPM vinyl records. So, many mike men still purchase this new brand since it works well with the 78 RPM vinyl records. I use the Sharp turntables, and one of those costs roughly \$3000." As he played at the cooking night, there was a specific style, flair, and individuality with which the mike man executed his duties. For example, many people admired the dexterity and panache with which he lifted the arm of the record player as he replaced the records on the turntable. Coupled with his unique style was his uncanny ability to play songs that pleased his audiences and those factors endeared the mike men to the people.

While the mike man was adept at selecting appropriate film songs for the Hindu wedding, he encountered some difficulty in providing the same level of service when he played at Muslim or Christian cooking nights. Kissoon admitted that there were some relevant Indian film songs related to Muslim

Record Players or turntables used by the mike men in the 1950s and 1960s.
Some of them are still in use today.

A mike man's ensemble on the back seat of a car during roving announcements.

weddings but limited numbers that applied to Christian weddings. This was because most Indian movies focused on Hindu weddings and therefore most of the songs reflected those scenarios. However, the mike man often made up for this since he had an extensive repertoire of Hindi film songs and which were loved by all audiences.

Indian Filmi Playback Singers

Since its introduction, playback singing has become the lifeblood of Indian movies. Professional playback singers recorded songs, and actors and actresses lip-synced those songs during the picturization or filming of the songs. This was done in such a professional manner, there was no noticeable dissonance between the audio and the lip- synchronization. Two of the finest filmi playback singers were Lata Mangeshkar and Mohammed Rafi, whose voices were instantly recognized everywhere by Indian filmi fans and who formed the core of the stock in trade Indian film songs for the Trinidad mike men.

The institutionalization of playback singing in Indian films became a reality after 1935 and provided many opportunities for the creativity and geniuses of not only the music composers, but the lyricists, musicians, music directors, and the playback singers to blossom. Many local Indian filmi fans went to see Indian movies because of the songs. The playback singers seemed to sell and sustain the movies with their songs, and similarly, it was no different for the mike men of Trinidad who played those songs up and down the countryside and made them part of the Indian cultural landscape. Many Indian movies owe their success to the playback singers and musicians since mediocre movies such as *Dil Dekhi Dekho, Silsila,* and *Junglee* with inferior storylines became successful because of the popular songs. It did not matter to the local Indian audiences that an Indian movies had a very poor storyline, so long as the songs were catchy, melodious, rhythmic, and brought that 'Indian flavor' to their ears, they fell in love with those songs, hook, line and sinker. With time, the mike men came to know and understand their audiences and selected songs they knew would create an impact with such audiences.

Sitahal maintained that it was very pleasing for a mike man when he played a song to hear members of the audience echo "that is song fadder(father); mike man that is song; mike man play that song again; yuh cyar get better than that—mike man take the belt; yuh know how long I waiting to hear that song and mike man you is the boss."

In Trinidad, Indian playback singers such as K. C. Dey, Saigal, Suraya, and Shamshad Begum were very popular in the 1930s and 1940s, but in the 1950s Mohammed Rafi, Mukesh, Lata Mangeshkar, Asha Bhosle, Mahendra Kapoor, Hemant Kumar, Manna Dey, and Kishore Kumar took over and dominated playback singing in the industry for the next few decades and provided the mike men with a treasure trove of Indian filmi songs to ply their trade.

With the coming of Indian programs on radio in Trinidad in 1947, those singers became more popular, and their songs were on the lips of all lovers of

Some of the favourite Indian Playback singers whose songs the mike men played.
From L to R: Mohammed Rafi, Lata Mangeshkar, Hemant Kumar, Asha Bhosle, Manna Dey, Mukesh, Kishore Kumar and Mahendra Kapoor.

Indian movies and Indian film songs. Mohammed Rafi and Lata Mangeshkar dominated this period, the Golden Era (1949-1969), and to some extent, so did Hemant Kumar, Asha Bhosle, Manna Dey, and Kishore Kumar. In later years, singers such as Alka Yagnik, Kumar Sanu, Udit Narayan, and Sonu Nigam made their mark in the industry and became very popular among the younger generation of the 1990s and beyond but they were not very popular with the mike men who preferred to play the songs of the 1950s and 60s.

Usually, the Indian film songs were known and popularized in Trinidad before the movie was released. In the 1950s and 1960s, before an Indian film was released in Trinidad, the local record shops received advanced 78 RPM vinyl sample records of the songs from the movies. The record shops sent messages to the mike men to visit the record shop for a copy of a new song from a new film. The record labels were color-coded. The blue label record was usually a sample copy, while the red or orange label records were for sale. The mike men were given the blue label record, and they popularized the songs throughout the country, wherever they went to play, and this helped to boost the sales of the records and popularized the movie before its release in Trinidad. [24] Two of the major record shops in the early days of Indian movies in Trinidad were Razack's Indian Records in San Juan and Balroop's Record Shop in Arouca. The songs were generally released to the mike men between six months to one year before the movie was released on the island. When radio and television became popular, the songs were then popularized through those media, but the mike men continued their work throughout the land playing their songs everywhere they went. The mike men held a unique appeal to the people, especially in the rural communities, and wherever they went, they always had an audience.

Ralph Narine stated that "the mike men were essentially collectors of Indian film songs. They made every effort to keep up to date with the new Indian songs brought into the country and used every available avenue to get a copy of those vinyl records. I can tell you from personal knowledge that there was a lot of competition, I should say friendly competition among the mike man themselves to get the most popular and best-loved Indian movie songs. If a mike man heard that one of his fellow mike men had in his possession a song that the people loved, a song that he wanted to make part of his collection, he would go out of his way to acquire a copy of that song either from the record shop or from private persons.

"Needless to say that many of the private persons who held copies of such records were very unwilling to part with them and only agreed to sell such records to the mike man for a negotiated price, which was usually way above what was paid for the original record. I have known mike men to pay exorbitant sums for records they did not possess, but it was their way of embellishing their stocks and keeping up with the demands of the market. For a mike man, it was an emotional thing for a fan to ask him to play a popular song such as 'Suhani Raat' from Dularie, and his reply was in the negative. Every mike man sought to please his host and his audience, and so as the years went by, the competition to acquire his stock in trade (78 RPM records) became keener. But that is not to say that they did not remain friends. Sometimes if a mike man had a job and one of his mike friends did not have to play out for that weekend, he would borrow records from his friend and return them after the job at no cost. Then again, I have known mike men who accompanied their mike men friends on a weekend job once they were free. That was their life, and despite their close friendliness whenever they met at weddings, they would still have friendly 'sound-off' battles between themselves, and the next day, they could be seen having a friendly drink in the neighborhood rum shop.

"But yes, the playback singers of India–of the Indian movie industry, provided them with the sounds and music they needed to entertain the audiences. And when they made selections to play at cooking nights or other avenues, they did so with a higher level of intelligence mixing the songs in such a way that audiences never became bored with listing to the music from the mike. There is no doubt in my mind that as far as the Indian film songs were concerned, these mike men were very knowledgeable in that field and were able to make selections to play based on their knowledge of the audience, requests from the host and requests from members of the audience. Every audience had their favourite Indian film playback singers that included Hemant Kumar, Manna Dey, Mukesh, Lata Mangeshkar or Mohammed Rafi. "[25]

Narsaloo Ramaya, who was himself the leader of the Naya Zamana Indian orchestra, indicated, "by far the most popular Indian film playback singer with the mike men and with local audiences was Mohammed Rafi. There is no doubt that wherever the mike men went to play, the Mohammed Rafi songs were the most requested and the most popular. It was the same with us in the orchestra business. Lata Mangeshkar and the other playback singers were popular, and of course, people requested songs by some of them, but largely, Rafi always topped the list. I think that Rafi was popular because he had a range of songs that the other Indian playback artistes did not have. And even in my orchestra, people always asked for the Rafi songs more than any other playback singer."[26]

25   Ralph Narine. Personal Interview. Port of Spain. 07/06/08
26   Personal Interview Narsaloo Ramaya. San Juan.05/05/08

Mike men preparing the stage for battle

CHAPTER 4

The Mike Men Sound-offs

"Mike men from throughout the country participate in these competitions and in so doing, help to keep the tradition of the mike men alive and well." Shaheed Mohammed.

As time went by and the new boxed public address systems took hold in the public domain, the mike man's presence at cooking nights dwindled, but he continued to hold an important place at the Sunday weddings where he led the dulaha's entourage to the dulahin's home. Also, he continued to maintain a nostalgic place among the older folks who loved to listen to the oldies filmi songs. However, despite their dwindling numbers, they continued to meet and keep alive their art form and the mike tradition.

Originally created to bring music for Indian weddings, currently they stage weekly playoffs at Preysal Recreation Ground tucked away in the rolling landscape of the central cane fields with its lush green surroundings. These men who "pit their sound systems against each other, blasting what they call back-in-time Indian oldies and Bollywood playback songs from the 1950s and the 60s from 78 RPM records" in Sunday battles, were "inspired by the Jamaican Dancehall clashes and the early hip-hop sound system battles in the Bronx." [27]

Kissoon noted that most of the mike men love to put a name to their system and the names are etched on the inside of the wide end of the horns. This could be grouped into two categories personal names and pseudonyms.
  Some mike men named their systems after themselves and their sons for example, *Sonny Boy and Sons, Maraj and Sons, Balo and Sons, Ravi, Timol, Imtiaz, Sharma, Andy, Satie and Son, Anil Sounds, Ramsamooj, Caltan Sounds, Ralphie and Sons, Bobby, Pawan, Shyo, Ricky, Harry and Sons, Chand and Son, Mohan and Kagee.*

Others, however, gave their systems names that were supposed to reflect the power, intent and dominance of the owner to convey a message that struck terror into the hearts of other mike men. For example, *Tomahawk* conveys a clear message of battle; *No Mercy* conveys its own meaning; *Guns of Navarone* declares war while *Hurricane* is ready to blow away everyone. In addition, several mike men were called by their mike names for instance Harrypersad

---

27   (ref:facebookhttps://www.facebook.com/115266865249308/videos/10150343804009143/?channel_id_override=115266865249308 mike men of Trinidad)

Harrikissoon was more often called by his mike name *Toro* than his given name. Some battle ready mike men etched their mike names on their horns for all to see and comprehend : *Dragon, Tiger, Lion, Guns of Navarone, Mount Everest, Janglee, Yahoo, Thunder Hawk, Eagle, Thunderstorm, Skyhawk, El Toro, Mischief Makers, Tomahawk, Fire Storm, Hurricane, Bhoot, Hanuman, Cobra, No Fear, Pusher, Big Noise, De Whip, Tanka, Time Bomb, Slice, D'Brave, Toro USA, Prince, Playboys, Thunderbird, D'Hawk, Star Boy, No Mercy* and *Street Hawk*.

Some mikes with names

PUMSHER
PUMSHER
BIG NOISE
BIG NOISE
THE SOUNDS
THE SOUNDS
COBRA
COBRA
ANDY
ANDY
RAMSAMOOJ

CALTAN SOUNDS
strictly Rules
TANKA
TANKA
MOHAN
MOHAN

HURRICANE
378-2199
HURRICANE
378-2199
HURRICANE·MIKE·P.A
SHARMA
SHARMA
Mischief Makers
ANDY
ANDY

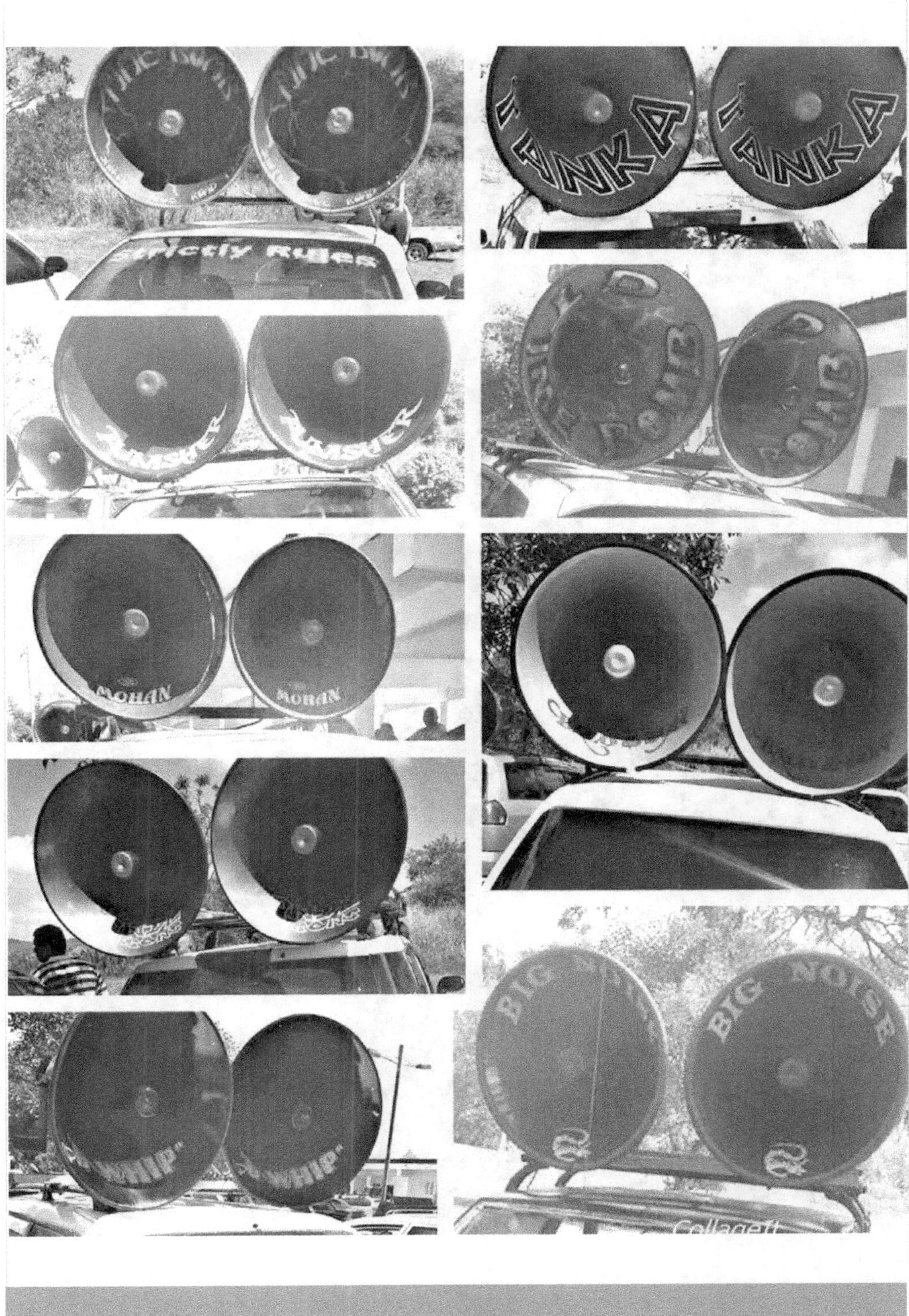

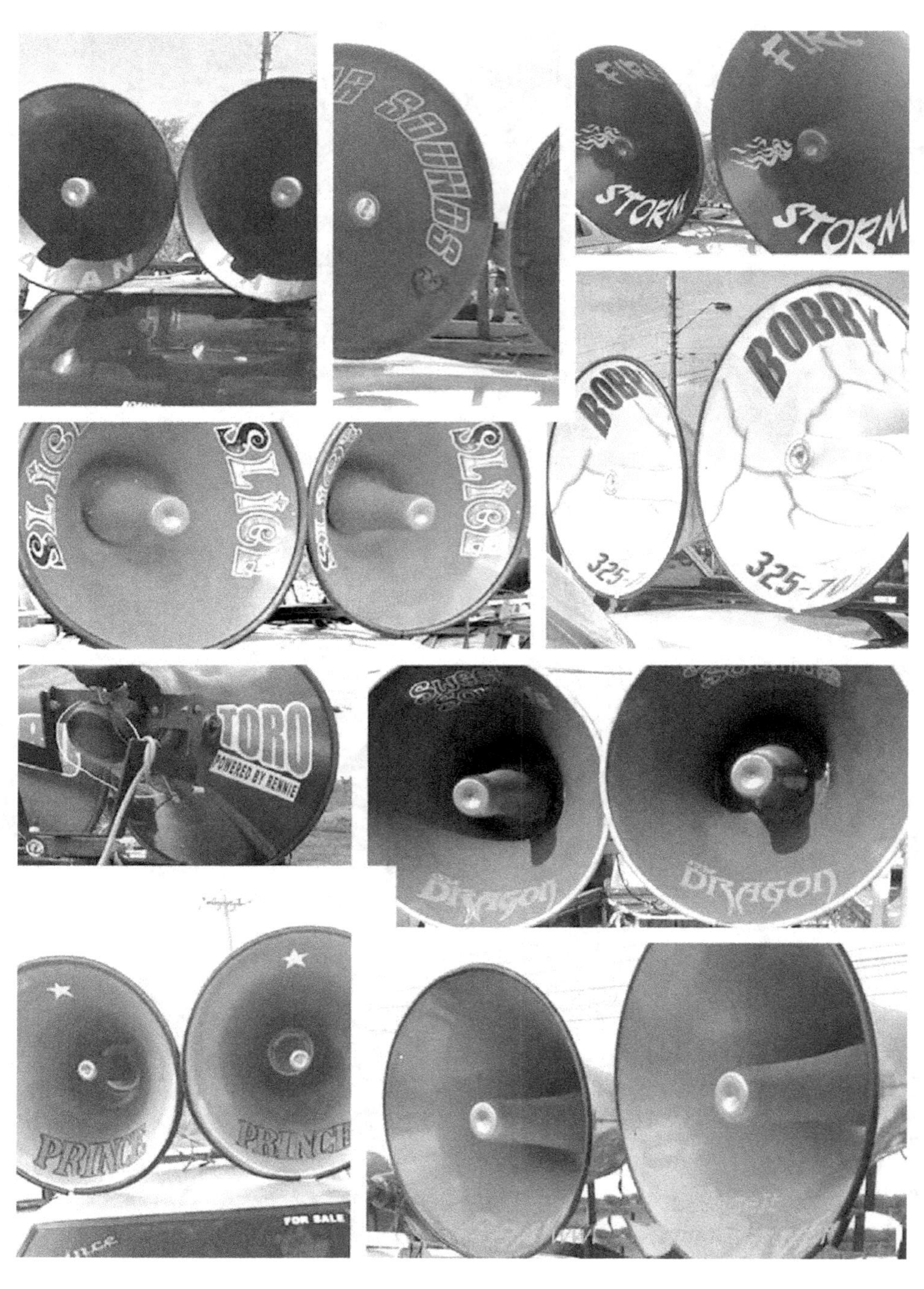

Ishmael Hoosaney, who went by the mike pseudonym of *Street Hawk*, indicated that 30 years ago, he was "the prime mover and organizer in the first Indian Arrival Day Sound-off Blast Competition in which the first prize was $25. Several mike men gathered and competed against each other for the entire day until, in the afternoon, the judges declared the winner. Not everyone was happy with the final winner, but they all accepted it as the judges were mike men like themselves, their peers. The next year the prize money was increased to $50 and then gradually to $200, but then the mike men decided that they wanted more than money, they wanted a keepsake–they wanted a trophy, something that they can show to their friends, their families and be placed in a prominent spot in the living room to show to all visitors that they had won the mike man competition. So, for the last 25 years, each year at the Indian Arrival Day Sound-off Blast Competition, the mike men vie for trophies in different categories of the competition since the competition has been expanded to include different areas of the mike system ensemble. Also, throughout the year, there are several other mike competitions such as the one which I attended on 25 January 2020 at Preysal."

Shaheed Mohammed, Assistant Secretary of the Mike Men Association, explained the competition in these words, "the mike competition is based on two-some mike-face-off against each other. The two mike systems are established 20 feet on either side of the judges. This is well measured and demarcated by mike men themselves. Three judges are chosen to judge the competition between these two mike systems. The judges are mike men themselves, but none

Shaheed Mohammed announcing competitors for a sound-off competition in February 2020 at Preysal Recreation Ground.

of those judges are participants in the current category being judged. Some are retired mike men who lend their services for the occasion. The judges are enclosed within a makeshift scaffold enclosure placed between the two mike systems, as seen in the picture below. Judging is based mainly on loudness and clarity. One judge is chosen by each of the competing mike men while the other judge is selected by the organizers of the competition.

"There are several rounds of the competition, depending on the number of entrants in each category. The categories are based on the number of batteries being used by the mike system. In today's competition (25/1/20), there are two categories: one is based on five batteries while the other is based on six batteries. "Each round of the competition consists of two mike systems competing against each other. The winners once again pull numbers to compete against each other in that category. At the end of that round, the process continues until two finalists are arrived at for the final competition. The winner of that final round is the winner of the category.

"To participate in the competition, mike men must pay a registration fee, which allows them to participate in a particular category. Each category that a mike man wants to participate in, he must register for that category and pay the requisite registration fee. Mike men from throughout the country participate in these competitions and in so doing, help to keep the tradition of the mike men alive and well. Trophies are awarded for the 1st, 2nd and 3rd place winners."

On the day of the competition that this researcher witnessed, some of the popular songs played by the mike men in their duels were: *Bidhi Ka Vidhan* (God's law) from the movie *Veer Bhimsen* [Life of Bhim] (1964); *Suna Suna Laage* (The Place Feels Empty) from *Neel Mani* [Blue Jewel] (1957); *Ek Musaphir* (A Traveler) from *Door Ki Awaaz* [Voice from Afar] (1964) and *Koi Laakh Karein Chaturai* (Be Compassionate to your Enemies) from *Chandi Pooja* [Worship of the Goddess Chandi] (1957).

In top and bottom pictures Judges stand inside the ramp between two mike systems listening to the blast to give their verdict on which is the better mike outfit.

Mike systems, each 20 feet from the center of the judges ramp
where the judges stand to listen to them play.

Judges pose for a picture before a mike sound-off contest at Preysal Recreation Ground.
L to R: Randy Kissoon; Khamraj Chotkana (Raj) and Gopaul Ramsamooj.

Hoosaney contended, "as in every sport, there can only be one winner, and the mike men accepted the judgment of the panel of judges as the panels comprised mike men like themselves, their peers.

"A mike man may take months preparing for a sound-off competition by practicing and upgrading his system, and when he gets down to the competition point on D-Day, there are so many things that could go wrong and cause a minor malfunction of the mike system. Additionally, having faced his competitors, he might have to admit that what he thought was a high-end system was, in fact, less in terms of power when compared to a few of his competitors. So, he might be a loser that day and accept it as a natural part of competitive life, but when he leaves the gayelle, he would be determined to return the next year better prepared, with an upgraded system, and would spend the whole year

70

preparing for the next major competition. And that's what keeps them going as they always try to improve and maintain their systems up to date."

While the mike men continue to play an essential role in the dissemination of information through announcements, election campaigns, and other events, this friendly group of men meets once a week, on Sunday evenings, at the Preysal Recreation Ground to do friendly battle over their mike systems. They gather from as early as 3 p.m. at the site to start their friendly 'sound-off' competition pitting each other's mike system against the other to determine who has the better mike system.

A regular mike system is loud and can be heard for almost three miles around. These men upgrade their systems using local technicians to make their mike systems sound louder and louder. Each one has a little secret of his own about what he has done to increase the output, quality, balance, and general efficacy of the system. They come prepared to blast away their opponents in a friendly clash that goes on for three hours or more. In the pictures below, see them lined up playing their music, awaiting their turn for the sound-off.

At these friendly clashes, other mike men like themselves, or retired mike men, are appointed judges (most times self-appointed), who take it upon themselves to judge these seeming amiable clashes. To launch the encounter, two vehicles are aligned facing each other about 20 feet apart with the mike funnels facing

Mike systems all lined up to take part in a friendly sound-off competition at
Preysal Recreation Ground in February 2020.

each other. They each play the same song, with the second one commencing a few seconds later. In the picture below, you can observe the mikes facing each other, and the judges are standing between the funnels absorbing the full blast of the mike listening to the sounds emanating from these huge funnels. The judges generally consider clarity and loudness as the main judging points. Randy Kissoon stated that the criteria for judging those sound-off clashes are cleanness or quality of sound, quality without distortion, power and loudness.

Mike face-off. Two mike systems face off at the sound-off competition in February 2020 at Preysal Recreation Ground with the judges standing between them.

The older, more experienced mike men take turns adjudging the mike systems on display. They are men of granite, eardrums seemingly made of some kind of metallic material. If you have ever been close-up to one of these mike funnels at full blast, your eardrums would probably split; they are so loud. This author had the opportunity to stand between the mikes at full blast, and he could not endure the extremely loud sounds for more than a few seconds. It was earsplitting. He felt like his eardrums would burst. His eardrums were vibrating in a way he had never experienced before because the sound was so loud. It was beyond him how the judges stood between those funnels, took the full blast of those sounds and walked away from it, seemingly unaffected. One mike man told him that they had grown accustomed to it, so it was easy for them, but to the newcomer, it could be difficult. During the afternoon, pairs of vehicles lined up against each other in this sacred procession of challenging each other for the unofficial title of Mike King of the Day. The mike men are a unique breed of men who take their work and entertainment seriously, and as they awaited their turn at the competition point, those on the periphery continued to play some of the beautiful oldies for which mike men became famous throughout the country.

Upgrades

The upgrading of a mike system can be an expensive undertaking as technicians are brought in to find innovative ways to increase the volume output yet maintaining clarity of sound, balance, and tonal quality. So, while

Sets of six batteries like those above are linked together in the trunks of vehicles for the sound-off competition

every mike man likes his mike to be at its loudest, this must not be done at the cost of enjoyment of the songs in terms of clarity. The sound coming out from the mike, from the funnels, must not be muffled in any way and must be at a pitch that it can reach people a few miles around. To power their systems, they employ several batteries. Some utilize two batteries, four batteries, five batteries and sometimes six batteries. These are motor vehicle batteries ranging from motor car batteries to truck batteries that can cost from $1000 to a few thousand dollars each, depending on the brand and whether it is a motor car battery or a truck battery. These batteries are linked together by a cable system that powers the amplifiers. The amplifier is key to the sound output, and so great care is taken to create a modified amplifier that can produce the power needed by the mike man. These amplifiers can cost thousands of dollars.

Anderson Bahaw, another mike man, noted "in the early days one simple amplifier was enough to power the mike system and most mike man used such systems but as time went by, and the need arose to overcome their friendly competitors, several mike men upgraded their systems to outdo each other and when they met at weddings,

Single input amplifier of the type used by the mike men in the 1950s.

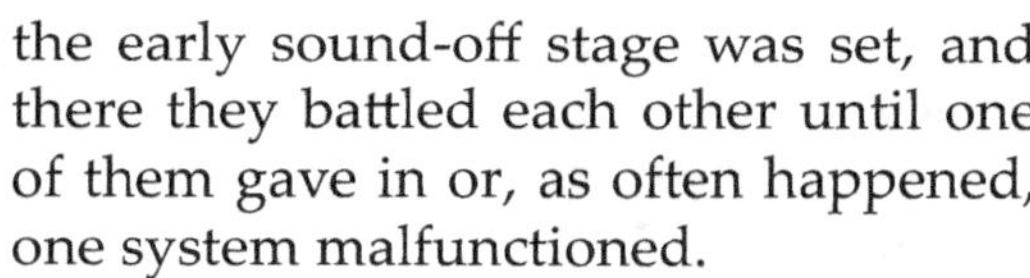

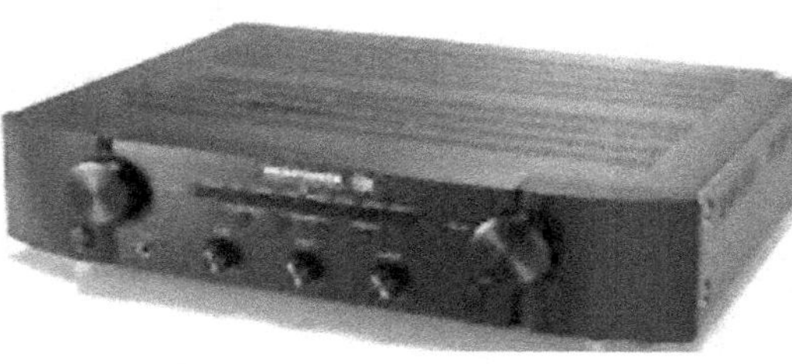

Later versions of the amplifier used by the mike men in Trinidad.

the early sound-off stage was set, and there they battled each other until one of them gave in or, as often happened, one system malfunctioned.

"The wedding battleground was the early sound-off stage for the mike men. It was a sight to watch and a pleasure to listen to these men do battle as they played some of the most beautiful melodies from the Indian film industry. That sound-off at the Sunday weddings set the stage for the creation of the Sunday sound-off competitions/ challenges that took place at various venues throughout the country." [28]

Ishmael Hoosaney, speaking to this researcher at one of the sound-off sessions at Preysal Recreation

____

28   Anderson Bahaw. Telephone interview,.17/10/19

Ground, explained that, "this gathering of mike man here today (13/10/19) is a coming together of mike friends to celebrate the victory of the mike man as a traditional aspect of our culture. They continue to survive and to be a major part of Indian culture and traditions in this country, even though now they mostly do announcements, political campaigns, rallies and Sunday weddings. But they remain an integral part of the

A mike man with his set-up of batteries, amplifier and 78 RPM Vinyl records in a motor vehicle.

Indian wedding scene, whether it is a Hindu, Muslim, or sometimes Christian wedding; they are the ones chosen to lead the wedding entourage from the boy's side as he journeys to the girl's side for the wedding and the return journey. During this journey, the mike men constantly play Indian film songs to the enjoyment of everyone."

Krishna Timol stated that the "sound-off competitions started as a Mike-o-Rama competition at the National Council of Indian Culture (NCIC) in the 1990s with Praimsingh as the main organizer and sponsor of that event. We won a trophy at that event. Since that time, we have always participated in Indian Arrival mike competitions, and I have a collection of more than 30

Two mike systems, Timol and Toro, face off at a sound off competition in Preysal Recreation Ground in October 2019. Observe the judges standing between the mike systems.

trophies that I have won over time." [29] Boodlal, however, stressed that "for me playing the mike and being part of the Sunday evening sound-off setting is a great stress reliever. If I feel stressed out or tired, whenever I play my mike system, or I reach the sound-off battleground, all my tiredness or my stress disappears completely. Besides, I get the opportunity to meet new mike men, those whom I did not know, and we can talk and share ideas about being a mike man. It is a great pleasure meeting and chatting with some of these mike men I had only heard about before. And of course, sometimes you have a little friendly sound-off, but as I said, I do not take part in any big competitions." On the other hand , Ricky Harrypersad, who became a mike man as a teenager, noted, "I attend the mike men gathering/sound-off sessions every Sunday evening at Preysal, and it is a very relaxing time for me. It is my hobby.

The trophy Ricky Harripersad won in 2018 at the sound-off competition.

"At last year's sound-off competition (2018), I won the first prize, and that's a great feeling. There is no money attached to the winner's medal. It is just the thought of knowing that you won the competition and have a trophy to prove it. It is a great feeling to know that your mike system is one of the best if not the best, having won this competition. "[30]

Randy Kissoon recounted that there are about 250 active mike men in this country, but that the majority are used for regular announcements while a fair amount are used for competitive sport.

Anderson on the other hand noted, "One of the things about being a mike man and participating in the sound-off competitions is the cost involved. Many of the regular mike men would like to participate in these competitions, but because of the cost of the batteries, they shy away from it, for example, the battery can cost about $3500, and several of the mike men tend to use between three and six of these batteries for these competitions, so if a mike man is using six batteries, that is roughly $20,000. And these mike systems are not used for public announcements or hired jobs. They are mainly for competitions and for most of the mike men this is a hobby. It is a relaxation time for most of us. It is a time when mike men can meet their friends and, put on show, their systems.

29   Krishna Timol.Telephone interview.14/10/19
30   Ricky Harrypersad,Couva. Telephone interview.21/10/19

"To modify a system for the mike competition, the mike man employs a mike technician adept at this kind of mike- work. Each mike man has his team of technicians, but that is not to say that one technician does not work for more than one mike man. We all have our teams, and we try our best to modify our systems to produce the best sound possible."

For some mike men, however, the idea of competing, winning or losing may take different perspectives as Rooplal Boodlal explains, "I have only taken part in the sound-off competitions once, and after that, I stopped. I was not happy with the results, so I decided not to participate, but that did not prevent me from being there and looking on at the competition after that disappointment. "Sometimes you might put out so much money to establish a mike system with such powerful batteries, and because of maybe inexperience or for other reasons, by the time you play your second song, the driver units might blow, and that's the end of the competition for you. So besides putting out that money, one has to be very careful in how you play the system. Sometimes the system might also overheat and cause other problems.

"We as mike men, we put out all this money to modify our systems to make it the best because of our love for the art form, because of our love of the traditions of the mike men and for just being mike men. You cannot make money out of this. The mike competitions only give you trophies. No cash. So the incentive for putting out this money is to make sure that the system is one of the best and the satisfaction of knowing that you can blow away your competitor. Furthermore, I must say that all mike men are friends and there is no hostility, but of course, we are not always satisfied with the results, but that does not prevent us from being friends and meeting up again the next Sunday to blast off.

"The thing about being part of the Sunday evening sound-off competitions is that it's a friendly clash, and most of us go there for the fun of it. But when two mike men clash, and the judges announce that Mr. X has a better mike, the loser or to put it better, the man coming second goes home and prepares his system with new modifications and comes back the next week better prepared to target the same individual to blast away–all in friendly glory. It's really a great thing to see how they challenge each other. As I said earlier, when the results are announced, not everyone is happy, but we accept the results and leave quietly intending to return the next competition day better prepared." [31] However, on a similar note regarding attending such sessions, Balgobin noted, "Every Sunday I am at the Preysal Recreation Ground for the Sunday sound-off friendly clash. I do not miss it. I enjoy going there because it's very relaxing, the atmosphere is full of camaraderie, and it's a stress reliever. I work during the week, and on a Sunday, I participate in the sound-off gathering of mike men. Being there and participating in those friendly clashes helps to relieve my stress completely. Once I attend that event, I am good to go for the rest of the

<hr>

31   Rooplal Boodlal, Barrackpore. Telephone interview. 14/10/19

week. At the sound-off, I also get the meet the many other mike men like myself, and we discuss matters relating to the mike business. It's really a very pleasant time, a very enjoyable time being there and mixing with other mike men. It's like a big family meeting every weekend, and there's a lot of comraderieship despite the sound-off or the blastoff between mike man. But these are friendly clashes, and we all accept the judgment of the judges who are mike men like ourselves.

"Being part of that sound-off setting allows me to get more experience in the mike business, understand how other mike men operate, and it encourages me to modify my system to meet the challenges at the sound-off competitions. It is there that a mike man gets to see what other mike men are doing and so he can compare his system to others and know if he needs to upgrade or maintain his system."

The friendly sound-off challenge begins like this. The mike men are all lined up and they play their mikes for fun and entertainment as other mike men listen. But it is not all fun as the playing of the mike is a call for action from a challenger. Suddenly one mike man from the line breaks rank and lines up against a potential rival facing the other mike man in the line. No organizer actually says who is the challenger or who is being challenged. The mike men themselves decide who they want to challenge. Sometimes, without even a word being spoken, a mike man may move his car from the line and park 15 to 20 feet opposite the mike man he wishes to challenge. The other mike man has to accept the challenge, and so they play the songs according to prearranged rules. Self-appointed judges, the experienced mike men, stand between the two mike systems on the turf as the two systems simultaneously play music at full blast. The judges turn and angle themselves to get the sound from different angles during the playing of the songs. Both mike men must play the same song. The challenger plays the song, and the one being challenged begins playing the same song seconds later, so the judges can hear the same song being played on both systems, each with a delayed play. In that way, they can hear clearly what is being played by both mike systems.

As an example of what goes on in the gayelle and the friendly rivalry, V J Sankar posted the following on Bahaw's Facebook page on January 6, 2019:
"One of my dreams was fulfilled in Preysal today. I am contented now. Thanks to the support from <u>Anderson Bahaw,</u> <u>Rakesh Boodram</u> and <u>Shiva Bhagoutie</u>... Today a small Jassle took place with some of the nicest songs I have heard down there in a while. No big guns though. A guy reversed behind me and, well, the rest was pure clean fun. We played about 5-6 songs against each other until my amp decided to overheat and trip. But today indeed was a really really nice day out on the field. I thoroughly enjoyed playing those songs for a change. Thanks again, guys. You all surely made my evening."

Anderson Bahaw gave a historical perspective of the friendly mike competitions when he stated: "the sound-off competitions that we see today has a long history going back to the 1950s and 60s. When mike men from the boy's side carried the wedding to the girl's side there was always a mike system there on the girl's side, and when these two mike men met up, there was always a challenge, a battle, but all friendly to see whose system was the better one. That continued for years, and sometimes it used to be a North-South battle or an East-West battle or a central vs. north or south battle depending on which part of the country the boy lived.

"The most significant, most popular mike man competition–sound-off competition–is held on Indian Arrival Day. Because of the many entries for the competition, it is held over two weekends preceding Indian Arrival Day. Contests begin at about 10 a.m. and go on until 6 p.m. There are several categories for the competition. Some groupings are determined by the number of batteries used, for example, two batteries, three batteries, five batteries or six batteries. The other judging criteria in the categories are set based on several factors, but for each group, trophies are awarded to the winners. We get sponsors to underwrite these trophies."

When a mike man got a job at a wedding, he was always curious to discover who would be playing on the other side and usually prepared for that clash, selecting some of his best records for the battle. One of the positive outcomes of those clashes was that the people enjoyed the friendly encounters because some of the best songs were played during the matchup.

As jobs for the mike men became scarce, some of them began gathering in open areas such as the cane fields to do battle there among themselves. So, they attracted gatherings and looked for a place to do their battles, a new battleground place, at recreation grounds and other areas until some years ago they settled on the Preysal Recreation Ground which is still being used.

Bahaw noted, "I attend the sound-off gathering of mike men every Sunday. It is a part of me. It is a great relaxing time for me, and I don't like to miss it." However, participating in a sound-off gathering exhibition takes time and preparation. Mike men from as far as Barrackpore, Penal, Rio Claro, Tableland, Princes Town, San Fernando, Sangre Grande, Rousillac, Cedros, Diego Martin, Gasparillo, and other parts of the country travel several miles to get to the sound-off site at Preysal in central Trinidad. It is the largest gathering of mike men except for the big competition days. Manoj Pariag of Chaguanas, who attended a few sound-off sessions as a member of the audience, indicated: "it is such a pleasant sight to see these mike men or rather all the mike cars lined up stretching into the distance. At any one time, several of the mike men played their mikes at the same time, and as you walk along, you can hear them at your leisure. If you hear a song that you liked very much, you can stand there and listen to that song and then move further on listening to another mike man play. I am accustomed to seeing two or sometimes for the most three mikes in one place. I have never seen so many mike systems in one place. When I used to go to cooking nights in the 1960s, I always wanted to get close to the mike man to talk to him, just to say hello to him or to ask him to play one of my favourite songs. But seeing so many mike men together in one place was really a treat for me and I am sure others as well. It is a pity not many people from the public attend these mike men gatherings. I think the mike men need to do a lot more to publicize these events. Looking at it, I'm sure that these men take a lot of time and effort to prepare the systems, prepare a car and select their songs to play at the sound-off sessions, and I don't think enough people come out to listen and appreciate what these mike men do."

Regarding the preparation for the sound-off sessions, Darren Basdeo added: "before going to the sound-off on Sundays the mike man must prepare because when he goes there, he will meet friends/competitors who are well prepared so he must make sure that he is also well equipped for the competition. Preparation includes testing and ensuring that the driver units are working well; that the batteries are tested and working at optimum level; the battery terminals are clean and can deliver the power required; that the record player or turntable is serviced and performing well with new batteries as well as backup batteries for the record player and that the amplifier is serviced and working well. In addition, the mike man must also make sure that his motor vehicle is in good working conditions depending on the distance he has to travel to get to the competition site."

At the sound-off sessions this author attended, he noted that all the mike men present used the old-time turntables with the 78 RPM vinyl records for the sound-off as Basdeo explained, "although there is no rule regarding whether one can use a CD or flash drive, most mike men prefer to use the older record players for this purpose. The true mike man, even today, prefers to use the 78 RPM vinyl records, which are spun on the record players. It's a lot easier for a mike man to record those songs on a CD or a flash drive and then play them, but there is a certain flair, a certain charm in operating the record player, changing the record or just flipping the record to play the other side, for each record has two songs, one on either side.

"My father, Lakhan Basdeo, aka Popo, was one of the better-known mike men in the business and won several competitions. I have a lot of trophies my father won in his time. Most people considered him one of the best mike men with some of the best production coming out of his mike system. But that did not come easy. That came with a lot of preparation and a lot of hard work and making sure that the system was always working at an optimum level and always properly tuned by Boy, Hublal Ramkissoon."

Krishna Timol, one of the older mike men in the business still around compared the preparations and the modifications needed to transform a regular mike system into a competitive system to a racing car, "I must point out that just as in the racing car community with racing cars people take the cars and modify

Trophies won by Lakhan Basdeo (aka Popo) and his sons Dale and Darren
at various Sound-off competitions. Lakhan's picture is inset.

them in different ways to produce a racing vehicle. Similarly, mike men
modify their systems–the amplifier and other components–to bring them up
to requirements for sound-off competitions. The conventional mike systems
cannot compete with these upgraded mike creations. And modifying the
systems can cost a lot of money, which the mike man puts out and never gets
back in terms of returns. He does it out of love as a hobby."

To explain the difference between the regular mike systems and the enhance ones, Timol further added: "Let me state that just like with a motor car if a motor car is modified for racing purposes, you will never find the owner using it to work taxi or to drive around the place on a regular basis. In a similar way, when the mike man modifies his mike system for competition purposes, those systems are not used for road announcements. We have special normal or regular systems set up for that purpose. So, every mike man who takes part in the sound-off competition produces a modified system that can cost between $40,000-$60,000. In addition, he may also own a few conventional systems for routine announcements.

"I can safely say that almost all the mike men who participate in the mike men sound-off gathering do it as a hobby and more so out of love for the art form and to keep the mike business alive. It is only when we gather at the sound-off location, we realize how many mike men there are in different parts of the country helping to keep this traditional art form alive. Most mike men like to have a name emblazoned on their funnels. In my case, it is Timol."

Some parts that are used in the modifications are difficult to come by and so they cost extra money. Continuing along the same line, Timol added, "the pair of funnels that you saw on show last Sunday (10/11/19) at the sound-off gathering was a gift from my father when I was 16 years old, and that has remained with me all these years. It still looks new because of the care that I take with it. That pair of funnels has played in places throughout this country at cooking nights, road announcements–you name it I have been there. Those funnels have been there and performed well and are still performing at an optimum level. The material of which those funnels are made are very durable and lasting and can last a mike man a whole lifetime and he can even pass it on to his children."

Long and short funnels

Speaking about funnels, Timol explained the differences between the short and long neck horns: "there are advantages and disadvantages between these two types of funnels. The main difference between these two sets of funnels is that the short ones tend to give you a better quality sound and that's why those short ones are used in the sound-off competitions. The long funnels, or to be more precise, the long neck horns carry the sound for long distances that can span between two to five miles or more. So, for road announcements where you want the message to carry far and wide, the mike men use the long neck funnels. That is why in the early days of the mike men in the country, most of them used long neck funnels.

"Funnels can cost a lot of money depending on the brand. The funnel I carry, the short ones, which you saw at the sound-off last Sunday (13/10/19), presently cost between $16,000-$20,000 per pair. They are the most expensive on the market. At the time when my father bought them for me at Ramkissoon's in

Shiva Bhagoutie (deceased) poses with a pair of long neck mike funnels.

Rio Claro in the 1960s, he paid $595.00. Now a similar pair can cost between $16,000-$20,000.

"The long neck funnels can be had for about between $2000 to $4000 per pair locally, if it can be bought from another mike man as a used one. But if it

Long neck and short neck mike funnels.

has to be imported from London, the same long neck funnels–the Grampian brand–can cost about $10,000 per pair. The cost can even go up to $15,000 when transportation is added. The Grampian brand is an excellent brand of funnels — the best on the market, and it is made in England."

Those funnels or horns are the most visible part of the mike system and must be kept immaculately clean, smooth and shining because the smooth surface of the horn is what allows for the least resistance when the sound waves leave the horn's neck — the shinier the surface, the better the quality of the exit sounds.

The sound-off gathering also made a significant impact on journalist Bavina Sookdeo, who, writing in the Trinidad Guardian (Tuesday, October 29, 2019) about the Sunday evening sound-off sessions quoted Vijay Kissoon, a former treasurer of the Trinidad and Tobago Mike Association, inter alia as follows:

"… the Mike Association existed for many years (over 40) but was formed under several other names. I have been involved in the mike business for almost 25 years…. In the past, we have gathered at Caroni, Debe and other places. We have been gathering in Preysal for about eight years now because we simply do not have a designated place to gather. What we do is just for the love of the mike, and we are really trying to keep the culture and tradition alive…..If there is good weather, we get about 20 to 30 mikes showing up, and we play music, greet each other, host a small meeting and discuss any issues that we might be having." Next, he continued, is the highlight of the evening, "we test out our systems and we have a little competition of our own. We play long time 78-pitch records–gramophone records. We mostly play old Indian songs. The competition is judged on whose mike plays the cleanest, sweetest and loudest music."

Sookdeo further noted "The Mike Men Association of T&T still perseveres and hosts family days, card competitions, fund raising events, choka and sada roti competitions and mike competitions every Indian Arrival Day. While the jobs which they get are few and far between, Kissoon admits that many people prefer the DJ system than that of the mike system."

But being a mike man is serious business, costly and takes up a lot of time. This is what some mike men had to say about being a mike man.

The Mike Men Speak…

Ricky Harrypersad, a mike man for many years who carries the name Ricky on his mike funnels, indicated that for his entire life as far as he could recall, he has always been involved in the mike business. His father and his grandfather

Ricky Harrypersad posing with his mike system at Preysal Recreation Ground during a sound-off Competition in February 2020.

Anderson Bahaw poses with his mike system before setting out on a road trip.

before him were mike men, and so he grew up with mike men and loved the mike and the sound that emanated from it. For him, it was natural, and it came naturally to him to follow in their footsteps and become a mike man. From a young age, he loved the music and the oldies songs played on the mike, and he indicated that he loved putting on the records on the turntable whenever they went out to play. He noted that "being involved in the mike business and playing the mike makes me happy. I do not do this for money. I do it because of my love for it, for the mike traditions, and because it is a form of relaxation for me. I love to hear the oldies songs. Playing the oldies songs on the mike brings out that special feeling not only of nostalgia, but a special kind of enjoyment that I get only from listening to the songs played on the mike system. Nothing else gives me that kind of enjoyment from listening to those songs. And I know for a fact that the songs played on the mike system hold an extraordinary appeal to lots of people who love to hear the songs on the mike. Most of the songs that are played are oldies from Indian movies from the 1950s and the 60s and part of the 70s. From my perspective, the most popular recorded songs that I have played on the mike system are the songs of Mohammed Rafi because members of the audience mostly requested those songs."

Anderson Bahaw, 30, one of the younger members of the Mike Men Association, stated: "I learned the mike business from my uncle Paul Boodhai, and I have continued the tradition of the mike business in the family. I am the only one in the family at present who has continued with this tradition. I took up the mike business because I found that that the tradition was dying out and as a young man in the village, in the community where I lived, I noticed that young people were not taking up this noble tradition of the mike man, so I took it upon myself to continue this tradition that my uncle kept alive for so many years, and now that he is not in the business anymore I decided to continue with it. From a very young age, I liked the mike music, and I was thrilled to listen to the songs, the oldies songs coming from the mike system. I only play oldies filmi songs on my mike system, and I found that people loved those songs, even many from the younger generation.

"In pursuit of keeping the mike men traditions alive and to reach out to the younger generation I founded a Facebook page called the *Mike Men Young Generation,* where I publicize lots of matters and pictures of the Sunday gathering sound-off sessions, and some of my posts on that Facebook page have gathered over 25,000 hits.

"My aim is to continue the mike traditions. Young people like myself in the Mike Men Association are gradually being called upon to assume more responsibilities in the mike fraternity as the older guys are leaving or becoming less active in the organization, so it is left to us in the younger generation to keep things alive among the mike men and to encourage young mike men to keep the traditions alive. I am the owner of seven sets of mike systems. Other mike men also have four or five systems, so I think that the mike men would be around for quite a while yet."

On the other hand, Darren Basdeo, who has been a mike man for 30 years, indicated that: "I became a mike man because of my father and my uncles who were involved in the mike business. My father was one of the best mike men in our community, and naturally, I became involved in the mike business with him from a young age. I was there with him everywhere he went to play mike. Being so close to him and being in his company at cooking nights and other events enabled me to get a first-hand understanding of the mike system, and I grew to love it, so I wanted to be a mike man like my father. It is part of my life, and I might say part of my genetic makeup.

"The most enjoyable thing for me in being a mike man is to play the songs, especially the oldies Indian film songs which audiences love so much. While I play songs by several playback Indian singers from the Indian film industry, the songs most commonly requested and most widely played by mike men and by me, are the songs by Mohammed Rafi. Songs by Lata Mangeshkar comes in second, but way behind the Rafi songs." Regarding the relationship between mike men, he added, "The relationship between mike men remains a very amiable one, very positive and very meaningful, and although we are in the same business and participate in competitions, our friendship remains intact. We often discuss matters relating to the mike business and sometimes even have arguments over points under discussion, but we never become enemies over the issue. We may disagree over things, but we don't vex with each other."

Dianand Balgobin, 39, who has been in the mike business since he was a teenager, noted that his father was a mike man, and from a very young age, he was also involved in the mike business with his father. Wherever his father went to play, he went with him and assisted him in various ways, including playing the records. It was a thrill for him to be part of that operation, so it was only natural for him to continue in the business. "It was as if the mike business was in my genes, so I naturally took over the business from my father."

Conversely, Krishna Timol, whose mike funnels carries his name 'Timol,' and who has been in the mike business for 47 years noted: "being a mike man came naturally to me since I was involved in the mike business from a very young age as my uncles owned several mike systems. I was about ten years old when I began going places with them, helping them operate their mike systems at cooking nights and other events. I was born into the mike business; I grew up in it, and I am still in it, and my sons are now part of it and continuing the tradition. My family owns several mike systems, but we have also become a crossover family who also owns a few box systems which my sons operate from time to time at weddings, parties and other events. But my first love has always been the mike system and will always be the mike system." Timol further noted that owning a mike system is a very costly business. Clearly, one can surmise that several of the mike men who continued the tradition of the mike system in the country grew up in the business either with their father or uncles and was highly influenced by those of the older generation operating their mikes.

Harrypersad Harrikissoon, who often returns to Trinidad from the USA to observe the mike sound-off competitions, remarked: "I was born into the mike family as my grandfather owned a mike system and I grew up to love it and became part of it. We played at cooking nights (in the south it is called farewell nights), weddings, funerals, temples, mosques, festivals such as Divali and Phagwa, political rallies. We also made announcements for supermarkets, cinemas, merchant stores and other businesses. One of the busiest times for us mike men was the election season when on mikes were utilized to the fullest by different election candidates from throughout the country.

"In my early years as a mike man, I played mike for several orchestras in the country, including Mellow Bugs, Gayatones and Naya Zamana orchestras. I used the same funnel systems for several years with the orchestras until the box systems came into play. So, in the early days of the Indian orchestras in Trinidad, they were beholden to the mike man to provide that operational mike system when they played at farewell nights. After many years of mike work in Trinidad, I migrated to the United States in 1996, but my mike system still goes on with the name of 'Toro USA' and continues to make its presence felt in the country. The tradition is continued by some of my great friends in the country who maintain and play my mike system. I even took a mike system to the USA

Harrypersad Harrikissoon of New York poses with his local mike system at Preysal Recreation Ground during a sound-off competition in February 2020.

and regularly play at several places, including temples and public events."
Krishna Dube, a resident of New York, indicated to this writer that he recently went to a Hindu wedding in New York in January 2020 where he encountered Harrikissoon playing his *Toro* mike system for the enjoyment of all at the wedding. Dube noted that 'Toro' played mainly oldies Indian film songs by Mohammed Rafi and attendees were very appreciative of that gesture. [32]

Regarding the upkeep of these systems and his history as a mike man Ismael Hoosaney, a mike man for 50 years explained: "I started playing mike since age 13. My father owned a mike, and from an early age, I assisted him from time to time, and eventually, I took over the mike business. One of my uncles also owned a few mike systems, and I must say that I always looked up to them both, my father and my uncle, and hoped that one day I would be like them owning a mike and playing to mike audiences everywhere. Years later, as it came to pass, I became the owner of not just one, but several mike systems operating throughout the country. I have been a mike man for almost 50 years now. I am also a mike technician, and I worked with a few mike men, including Imtiaz Ali, who won several mike competitions with my assistance as his technician." Imtiaz Ali explained:

"I have been a mike man for more than 25 years, but I have been with the mike since I was a young boy. I was born into the mike business as my uncle was a mike man and from an early age, I went with him everywhere he played the mike.

I am a mike man because I was born into it, and I love being a mike man. Being a mike man is a joy for me. While I enjoyed playing the mike at functions and on the road, the highest enjoyment for me and the greatest fun I get is at the sound-off sessions where we determine which mike is the loudest and the best. Specially enhanced mike systems which we call 'Moosar Mikes' (power mikes) are used in the sound-off sessions. I have participated in several of these sound-off sessions, and the Sunday evening sessions are all friendly clashes. There are several sound-off competitions each year, but the most important one is held on Indian Arrival Day. I have also won several sound-off competitions over the years."

CHAPTER 5

Maintenance and Upgrading of the Mike System

"The mike technician is one of the most valuable people in the mike industry, and he is the one who keeps the systems working and up to mark. Without his input, the mike men cannot compete effectively or efficiently in any sound-off competition." Randy Kissoon.

The upgrade and maintenance of a mike system is a very costly affair. Several mike men have had to get out of the business due to the high cost of the upkeep and various other factors, including the downturn in the economy and the diminished use of the mike systems at Hindu weddings and other social events. However, despite the cost of keeping the system working at its peak and upgrading those systems for the sound-off competitions, the mike men continue to be a force to reckon with in the country and the mike systems continue to be used for commercial and the political announcements.

In describing the modifications and final makeup of the system, Kissoon noted, "there are several factors that go into the modification or upgrading of a mike system. The mike system consists of an amplifier, a record player or turntable, driver units, funnels or horns, batteries, and the 78 RPM vinyl records played by the mike men. I might add that the final price of a high-end system may vary depending on the brand of batteries used, the type of amplifier, the record player and even the horns and driver units used in building or modifying the system."

Harrypersad further noted that his system costs more than $30,000 to alter and bring it up to competitive level while Darren Basdeo, who has been a mike man for over 30 years, claimed that his system costs around $50,000 after alterations. Basdeo quoted as an example the value of a modified system his father once owned, "my father had a passion for the mike business and owned one of the best modified, upgraded mike systems I know of in the mike business. He was offered $70,000 for it and refused to sell the system, and that was more than five years ago. Because of his love and his passion for the music and his emotional attachment to his mike system, he could not part with it for any amount of money. That system had great sentimental value for my father, and I would say that it is the same for most of the mike men in the business today. Many of us are in the mike business because of our love for it and because of sentimental values. "

In giving a breakdown on some of the costs associated with the upgrading and modification of his mike system Basdeo revealed: "the driver units that I use can cost about $1000 each, and each mike system carries four driver units (two for each horn), and we usually have a few backup ones in the event of failure because the diaphragm can blow very easily and it will cost about $300 to $400 to repair each. We usually keep a few of these units in reserve. Besides, I also use the large Caterpillar truck batteries with my system. These Caterpillar batteries are the best on the market. I tried others, but they soon failed. Some brands on the market, which mike men use are Track Mack, Power Master, and Caterpillar among others. Different mike men prefer different brands. I prefer the Caterpillar brand because those batteries give a better output and last longer. The cost of a Caterpillar battery from my last purchase was $3700 each. And I use five of those with my system. That is a cool $18,500 just for the batteries alone, not counting any backup batteries, and I usually have one or two as backups. Now we rarely get guarantees on those batteries because they are not attached to any particular vehicle, so the mike man takes a risk in purchasing those batteries.

"Most mike men also have battery chargers that are used to charge the batteries to prepare for a job or the competition. The battery chargers are an additional expense that can cost around $2000-$2500.
"We usually work those batteries on weekends for the sound-off clashes, so the batteries are rested during the week. Depending on how such high-end batteries are treated or used, a mike man can get between 3 to 4 years' service from them before replacing them. I love the Caterpillar battery because, over the years, I found that the Caterpillar gives better and longer service compared to the other brands. For me, no other brand can match the Caterpillar. It's a little expensive, but they work well. The Caterpillar batteries are maintenance-free. I use maintenance-free batteries because they tend to last longer."

Dianand Balgobin, 39, one of the younger mike men on the scene noted, like Basdeo, "the mike system is costly to modify and upkeep. Everything dealing with the mike system is expensive. I use the Caterpillar batteries from Track Mack because those are the best, although they are costly. Previously I used the Yuasa, Delco and other brands but had problems with them. I must explain that for the amplifier to operate at the optimum, the voltage-current being fed to the amplifier must be at a certain level. If it drops below that level, certain parts in the amplifier may be destroyed. In my experience, there were times when the batteries began to fade with the power being less than required, and because of that low voltage going to the amplifier, parts such as the ICs malfunctioned and had to be changed. In a few instances, the amplifier was completely destroyed. So, I switched to the Caterpillar batteries, and since then, I have not had similar problems with my system. I use five 33- plates Caterpillar batteries in my system. Each one cost $5300. So that alone cost $26,000. When the cost for modification of the amplifier is added with other minor costs, my complete system costs can average between $50,000-$60,000 total."

He further argued that it was essential to have backups for the significant components of the mike system, such as batteries and driver units, stating: "I must add that it is imperative to have reserves, especially when you are participating in the mike competitions. So, I usually have backup batteries, a backup record player, backup driver units, among other things. The driver units are usually the first to go, and, in my case, I change them myself. Recently I purchased a few of those driver units, each costing $1400. We normally like to have a few of those units in reserve. I have twelve extra units as reserves." He further added, "The main differences in modifications that are made to the high-end system is to produce louder and higher quality sounds. Being a mike man at the competitive level costs a lot of money, so a mike man who wants to maintain his status at that level must be prepared to spend his cash; otherwise, it becomes challenging to maintain a system and to participate in the sound-off competitions.

Some trophies won by Dianand Balgobin at Sound-off competitions over the years.

"I do this more out of love for the art form rather than to make money. Very few mike men make money out of this. Some mike men earn a living by announcing with the regular low-end mike systems, but these superior systems, like the one I own, are rarely used for day-to-day announcements." He further added that only specialist mike technicians are used in the upgrade of the amplifiers while Harrypersad corroborated, "and I can tell you, it can cost a tidy sum when we add the parts and labour involved."

Driver units for mike horns of funnels.

Imtiaz Ali noted that "as a mike man it is possible to make a comfortable living from the mike business, but you have to run it as a business and be committed to it. You also have to maintain your mike equipment and keep it in proper working condition. I chose this as a business, and it is how I make my living, but it also provides me with pleasure because I have other systems that I used for the sound-off sessions. The 'sound-off sessions is leisure time for me and for many of the mike men, for it is there that bonding takes place and where we rekindle our friendship and joust with our mikes and have fun. It is really a very pleasant time to be at the sound-off sessions on a Sunday evening. "Generally speaking, the regular mikes are used for announcements and the 'moosar mikes' (upgraded mikes) are used for the sound-off competitions, but sometimes a few mike men use the moosar mike to carry Indian weddings because of the loudness and the durability of the system."

Randy Kissoon, one of the top mike technicians in the business, explains further regarding an upgraded mike system not being used in everyday road announcements. To illustrate this point, Kissoon used an analogy of upgrading a motor car for competition. He noted: "let me demonstrate this point through an analogy you will readily understand. Let us take a racing car as opposed to an ordinary car. They are not of the same quality, although both have similar components. The car that is modified has higher quality parts and is regarded as being at the upper end while the other car has parts of the regular lower end prices. Those vehicles at the upper end of the spectrum are specifically remodeled or modified for racing purposes. Those cars will not be used for everyday driving while the regular low-end cars are used for that purpose. Similarly, with the mike men, the mike systems that are upgraded or modified are used specifically for sound-off competitions or for the Sunday gathering of friendly clashes while the regular mike systems are used for announcements and other routine works."

Krishna Timol, a mike man for over 47 years, noted, "an original amplifier comes in with one 500 output channel. In modifying such an amplifier, a mike technician usually changes the system from one output to two outputs. In upgrading the output channel, the technician can create a channel that can give output above 10,000 units. Also, some technicians can input as many as 50 additional transistors in the amplifier to 'supe it up' in the upgrade process. " Kissoon, explaining the task of the mike technician, further added: "In a sense, it is like the sound systems that some people install in their motor cars. They modify the systems to bring out a greater sound quality or to make it sound louder. In our case, however, the technician must make sure that it does not only sound louder, but that the sound is very clear and precise. It cannot be that the sound is loud and muffled; it has to be loud and clear, so a great balancing act has to take place there regarding the upgrade of the mike system, what the mike man requires, and the ability of the mike technician to create the product desired. That is no hit and miss operation. The mike technician is one of the most valuable people in the mike industry, and he is the one who keeps the systems working and up to mark. Without his input, the mike men cannot compete effectively or efficiently in any sound-off competition."

Mike Technical Services

Based on feedback from several mike men, the mike technician emerges as the critical factor in the upgrading, maintenance, and technical advice regarding the production and upkeep of the mike systems for competitive purposes. Harrypersad indicated, "each mike man has his technician who works with him and helps him develop his system according to his needs, especially for the sound-off competition. Developing a mike system like this is really a labour of love as we cannot earn money from it" while Rooplal Boodlal (aka Dollars), 66, argued "the technician is one of the most important parts of this whole establishment of being a mike man, especially a mike man taking part in the sound-off competitions. Without the technicians, the mike man would be at a complete loss to know what to do and how to organize his system. The mike technicians are a special breed of men who specialize in modifying systems to produce extraordinarily loud sounds from those mike systems, and the louder he could get a mike system to play, the better or more complex a mike technician he is regarded."

Kissoon, a mike man and one of the most formidable mike technicians in the business, agreed, noting: "the mike technicians are perhaps the most crucial part of the equation in the mike industry, particularly with the modifications and upgrading of mike systems that are used for the sound-off competitions. I cannot overemphasize the value and importance of the mike technicians' work in preparing mike men and their mike systems for the Sunday sound-off gatherings and the other competitive aspects of the mike man's operations in this country. It is because of the mike technicians' input into the mike industry that the industry is alive and kicking in the country today.

"These technicians are trained technicians in their fields, and they bring their skills to bear on the mike systems in helping the mike man to upgrade his system to produce a better quality, yet louder sound. Not all technicians can do this kind of work. So, these technicians, while they are general technicians, they are highly skilled in the aspect of the work they undertake with the mike systems such as the modifications of the amplifiers and other components. Largely, it is a balancing act by the technician to produce high quality sounds, yet higher dB without creating sounds that are muffled or in some way impaired. Many such technicians are operating in the field.

"The mike technicians are the ones who upgrade a system from being a regular mike system to a highly modified system that can produce sounds at some of the highest amplitude, and yet the sounds are clear, audible, distinct, and of a high quality with no distortion or dissonance. Each technician has developed his modus operandi in creating his final product, and these technicians work with selected mike men who keep them on their payroll indefinitely. Once a mike man is satisfied with the work of his technician, that technician stays with him and continues to repair, maintain, and upgrade the system as necessary." Kissoon went into further details on the work of the mike technicians adding, "there is no doubt in my mind that without the work of the technicians the sound-off gatherings and the competitions would have fallen by the wayside because every time two mike men clash at the sound-off get-togethers, each one leaves the scene with the intention to better his system for the next time and this is where the technicians come in. It is because of the work of these technicians the mike man can continue to compete at the highest level in the mike business.

"The mike man's technician does not focus on only one aspect of the mike system, but looks at the overall system, including the record player, the amplifier, the driver units and the funnels. It is only when the technician focuses on the entire system that he can produce the quality of sound required by the mike man to compete at the highest level.

Randy Kissoon makes a point to another judge, Gopaul Ramsamooj just before the commencement of the mike men sound-off competition at Preysal in February 2020.

"The mike technician's job is very critical in ensuring that the entire system operates smoothly as a unit. He must ensure that one aspect of the system does not override the others and cause a breakdown of the whole system. For

Mike Horns with more than one driver units.

example, in modifying an amplifier, the mike technician must consider the type of record player being used and the kind of unit drivers through which the signal must pass before being put through the funnels. Some horns use multiple drivers and all these factors must be coordinated in such a way that it can produce harmonious, continuous sound with no feedback or back pressure on the system.

"Now that is not to say that the mike technicians are not called upon to service and maintain the conventional low powered systems. Those systems also need servicing and may sometimes require minor upgrades depending on what type of work they are called upon to do. So, the mike technician works with any type of mike system to maintain them or to upgrade them as necessary. It all depends on what are the requirements demanded by the particular mike man. Some mike men prefer to keep their systems at the lower end to make public announcements while others keep their systems at the upper level to participate in competitions. The mike technician's input in maintaining both types of systems is crucial."

Another set of Mike Horns with more than one driver unit attached to each horn.

Regarding the components in the mike system that are changed when the system is being modified or upgraded, Kissoon stated, "some of the components of the amplifier that are changed include transistors, transformers, capacitors, and resistors but it is the technician who ultimately determines what and how many components are to be changed or added to give the mike man the power he demands."

Boodlal, on the other hand, in directing attention to the extent and cost associated with the modifications that can be performed on an amplifier system such as his system, explained, "with an average original amplifier being modified or upgraded to competition level the cost can be between $5000 to $7000 in labour.

During such modification of the amplifier, the technician may add up to 50 to 60 transistors and a few other components such as transformers into the system and rewire it accordingly. A transistor can cost between $50 and $60 each, while an original amplifier can cost around $5000 to $7000. Such an amplifier would normally have one 500 output channel and twelve transistors."

Kissoon, speaking about the work of the mike technician and what it takes to be such a unique person in the mike industry, noted, "The mike technician is not specifically trained to be a mike technician. He brings his technical abilities to the job and adapts his training to the new task at hand. It takes a lot of patience, time and serious technical work from the mike technician to perfect his job. The technician can spend days or sometimes more than a week in developing a high-end mike system, but after developing that system for his client, he must stay with the system to ensure that it performed as per his design.

"The technician cannot be satisfied with just upgrading a mike system and leaving it at that. He cannot only remain in a garage or a room and modify a system and be contented with that. He also has to go out on the field and develop a feel of what the competition out there is like and improve his system to surpass what the competitors offer. He has to play the mike system and pit it against others in the field to gauge its operational efficiency, and over time, make adjustments or add components to bring it to the point where the mike man is satisfied, and he is also satisfied with the product. That can take weeks or months at a time. "

Kissoon continued, "there are just about six specialist mike technicians in the country. They are Randy Kissoon, Ishmael Hoosaney, Khamraj Chotkana (Raj), Hublal Ramkissoon, Sunil and Ricky. There is no hostility between technicians. We are all friends, and we try to do our best to please our customers and to work according to our customers' demands. On the day of competition, when a mike man emerges victorious, that is a big plus for the mike technician and his client as well. Generally speaking, people in the field only see the mike man and the mike being operated. They hardly ever see the mike technician at work on the field because of the nature of his work since he tends to work very quietly in the background. Every technician works for a few mike men, and these mike men tend to stay with their technician unless they have reason to shift allegiance."

Speaking about the breakdown of systems during competitions, Kissoon further noted, "with regards to balancing the various aspects of the system, there are times, of course, when a system can suffer from overload and can overheat, and the amplifier might be put out of service. Sometimes too, the mike man might, due to over-exuberance, overrun the volume control beyond the limits of the system's capacity and would probably blow the diaphragms in the driver units. So, we as technicians, when we create the upgraded system, we usually warn the mike men about the limits and delimitations as far as operating the system is concerned. While every mike man entering a competition would like to win it, quite a lot depends on how the system is configured to produce the sounds that will eventually determine the winner. So, in the end, it is the technician who determines what components are to be added to the mike system to produce the required sound and whether it is sufficient to overcome the competition. Each mike man understands that there will always be mike systems that may be superior to his system and, realizing such, he will always want to upgrade his system beyond the capacity of his competitor, and that is what keeps the competitive mike industry alive in this country.

"In the old days, in the 1950s and 60s, people who owned mike systems were considered unique people, outstanding people, because it was a bit of outlay in terms of cash to purchase a mike system and maintain it. Whereas in the early days a mike system could cost between $500 -$1500, today things are a lot different, and a good mike system can cost beyond $25,000 or $30,000 but the image of the mike men is not as glorious as in those earlier times.

"However, because of the competitive nature of the business, most of the mike men, through the use of skilled technicians, have altered their systems and amplifiers and upgraded them to produce louder sounds, spending lots of extra cash in the process. They update their amplifiers to what, in the mike world is called 'racing amps' that use 24 volts, 36 volts or 48 volts as the case may be depending on their fancy and the range of sound they wish to advance to whether it is midrange or extraordinary advanced range. These upgraded systems can be heard for up to 3 to 5 miles around."

Each mike man has his modus operandi and produces the system as he sees fit. Such systems require constant maintenance, and so specialized mike technicians are brought in to keep the systems working and up to competitive level. At one of the sound-off competitions this writer attended, (02/02/20) all the mike systems on display were upgraded systems operating on 4 to 6 batteries. They were all considered high-end mike systems. Purchasing, outfitting, and maintaining a high-end mike system today is indeed expensive.

Despite these substantial expenses, the mike men do it more for the love of it because very few of them ever recover the money spent on such systems. However, some mike men still make a living out of the mike work through announcements and other events using their regular systems. This year (2019) and next year are election years, and election time is a very lucrative time for the mike man, but outside of that, he depends on weddings and announcements from businesses and government agencies such as the Trinidad and Tobago Electricity Commission and the Ministry of Health for specific announcements.

Mike systems galore, all lined up and waiting for the Sound-off Competition to begin

CHAPTER 6

Social and Political Impact

They communicated with the people, lived among them and played their music for their enjoyment. As with other aspects of their routines, the constant playing of Indian film songs kept those songs alive among the people, and in time, the songs became commonplace among them, and the mike men gained in status among East Indians.

While in the early days of their existence, the mike men were mainly popular among members of the East Indian community, their work was eventually noticed by other sections of the country and they were hired for several other activities including bazaars, sports meetings and announcements connected to politics and government services. Even though many people considered them "noisy and annoying," they eventually became the mouthpiece of many businessmen, politicians and government utility services. They performed valuable services in times of crisis to get information to the public promptly, and many people believed that it was due to the services of the mike men that many crises in the health sector were averted.

Political Campaigns

With the introduction of party politics in Trinidad and Tobago in 1956, mike men became an integral part of political campaigns by the parties in the election. Since then to the present time, the election season has been one of the most lucrative times of the year for the mike man. Although it was a short period, every mike system was utilized during an election campaign as candidates tried to gain the upper hand over their opponents and in some areas of the country, there were shortages of mike systems during the election campaigns. With political parties and independent candidates, the mike man was the best option to get their messages out to the people through announcements called "roving mike announcements" and through the use of the microphone at political meetings. Usually, the mikes remained on the motor vehicle while speakers at political meetings made their speeches on stage using the microphone provided.

In the early days of electoral campaigns, wherever the mike automobile went during the election campaign, the candidates were seen in the vehicle speaking to the constituents as they traversed the constituency. With the introduction of the cassette recorders, and later digital recordings, the politicians no longer needed to sit in the roving mike vehicle and speak to their audiences. He simply recorded his message on a cassette tape or CD and the mike man played this recording throughout the constituency.

In most cases, particularly in the early days of tape recorders, many people had no idea that it was a recording that was being played and thought that it was the candidate himself, who had come to the area with the mike to personally give his message to them. The social and political impact of the mike men was phenomenal as they worked not only in their traditional areas but in communities throughout the country. Through them, the politicians made contact with the people in remote areas in an effort to spread their messages and gain their votes at election time.

Throughout the political season the mike men were inclined to remain neutral. In some areas where there is a shortage of mikes for rent, one mike man might work for more than one political party. Alternately in other areas, one mike man might own more than one mike system and rent out his services to more than one political party. Ramash Ramsumair, an avid mike enthusiast and a political activist indicated that throughout his activist years he has found the mike men to be non-political.

Besides politicians, numerous government agencies and businesses regularly made use of the mike men to get their messages out to the people at short notice. For example, if there was an outbreak of malaria in a particular part of the country and there was a need for urgent spraying with insecticides, the Ministry of Health, Vector Control Division, utilized the services of the mike men to inform residents of the schedule for spraying in the areas affected. Similarly, within recent years, other utilities such as the Water and Sewage Authority (WASA) and the Trinidad and Tobago Electricity Commission (TTEC) utilized the mike men to inform residents of affected areas when scheduled works and interruptions of the utility services would negatively affect them.

Sale Events

By the 1960s, many business concerns began using the mike systems at their businesses and also hired them to go into villages and surrounding areas to publicize sale events at their commercial enterprises. The mike man went into the areas announcing the sale events and distributing flyers to residents. It is important to note here also that when making these announcements, the mike man played Indian film songs to draw the attention of the people. Often, most people were interested in hearing the Indian film songs played by the mike man rather than the announcements which he came to make. Harry Charran, who operated a family store in Chaguanas in the 1960s, indicated that he usually hired a mike system on weekends to make sales announcements at the store to attract customers and he was the chief announcer, inviting people to visit the store to see the bargains being offered.[33]

Death Announcements

A unique feature about the mike system was its ability to reach out to the public in a manner that other communication devices could not. The share loudness and carriage of the sound ensured that people within a wide radius were able to take note of the messages being broadcast. Also, the mike man

---

33   Interview with Harry Charran.19/05/17. Valsayn, Curepe.

went into areas where there was no electricity and broadcast his message to everyone. All within the catchment area heard the message simultaneously.

Besides those announcements, the mike men made their appearance during the death of a villager. From the inception of the mike man in Trinidad, many people realized that the quickest way to get the message of a death in the village to surrounding areas was through the mike man. In those days, when there were no refrigeration services to keep the deceased body for long periods, it was essential to get the word out as quickly as possible as funerals were usually held within one or two days after the death occurred. In those circumstances, the mike man came to the rescue and made death announcements in the village and surrounding areas playing Indian religious film songs between the announcements. Ramdeowar expressed the view that in those early days of the mike man it was considered "unjust and unwise" to charge the family of the deceased to make a death announcement so his contribution was generally accepted as community service and any mike man who asked for money in those days was frowned upon as trying to "take money from the dead."

Road Announcements

Krishna Timol, a mike man with vast experience in road announcements, indicated: "not every mike man knows how to make road announcements properly. Even those who can get private personnel to record announcements for them, do not 'perform' the announcements in the proper way. Very few people consider the various factors that affect announcements such as the wind direction, the movement of the car, and the distortion that occurs when the vehicle is in motion against the wind.

"Proper road announcement etiquette dictates that the mike car should come to a stop while the announcement is being made and when the announcement is completed, then should the mike car continue in motion and stop at a reasonable distance and continue with the notices. The mike man knows how far the system would carry the sound and so he would stop at reasonable intervals so everyone could hear the messages. "However, there are some mike men who continue to drive their vehicles while the messages are read out and that is a great disservice to the listening public because the people at one end of the street would probably hear the beginning of the advertisement or the announcement while the people at the other end of the street will hear only the end of the announcement. This is a great disservice both to the audience and for the people who contracted the mike man to perform such service. You are being paid to make an announcement, and it is understood that people should hear the announcement in order to make full meaning of it. It is difficult when one group of the people hears only the first part of the message and another section of people on the street hears the end of the announcement. Many people have complained about this type of activity by mike men. I have also received comments from people about such activities about other mike men. In my case, we try to be professional and make announcements in the proper way. So, in the mike business, there are certain etiquettes that a mike man should follow." It must also be noted that during the intervals between the 'stop and make' announcements, when the mike car drove to the next point to continue the delivery of the message, the mike men always played Indian film songs as a call to attention to the public. The songs seemed a beacon call to the next point when the car would stop, and the announcement made.

Some mike men stated that often several people were more interested in the songs being played and found the announcements an interruption to the melody being played.

Timol continued, "Along the same line of announcements, some mike men also drove very slowly while performing such duties and claim that by doing so, people could hear the entire announcement. But some announcements are relatively long, lasting a minute or two, and again some people only heard the beginning of it while others heard only the end. This is particularly important when announcing sales, death announcements or even health announcements because it is imperative that audiences get the full meaning of the announcement. As a mike man with many years' experience, I can tell you that people appreciate it very much when they can get the full import of an announcement."

Most mike men are not trained announcers, so they sometimes hire professionals to announce for them, but the cost associated with that can sometimes be exorbitant. In addition, instead of making live announcements many mike men today pay these professionals to do voiceovers or record the script and play these announcements on the road as they drive along. That is the reality of the announcements made today.

Despite those misgivings when it comes to making announcements for supermarkets, furniture stores, Ministry of Health announcements, political meetings, electioneering road campaigns/announcements, nothing beats the mike man. He is head and shoulders above everyone else in this business. While some people sometimes complain about the noise from these superb loudspeakers, many are happy to learn of bargains at supermarkets and stores and especially announcements that are made by the Ministry of Health regarding immunization and spraying for mosquitoes. Also, significant announcements are made by the electricity commission informing residents that electricity in the area would be turned-off on a specific date between certain times. These announcements are taken very seriously as people, once informed, prepare for those eventualities.

Timol further added, "a regular mike system that is used for announcements and routine jobs can cost in the vicinity of $15,000-$20,000."
When not making announcements, several mike men play the system at home for the enjoyment and the entertainment of friends and relatives who live in the vicinity. Balgobin noted, "on weekends, especially on the Sunday morning, I play the mike at home, and the people in the area enjoy listing to the music. If by 10 a.m. on a Sunday, I do not start playing the mike, some neighbors call and ask: Why you not playing music this morning? Many of them wait for that time to listen to the beautiful songs of yesteryear. I receive very good comments from friends and neighbors about that practice, and I am encouraged to play the mike on a Sunday morning so they can stay in their homes and enjoy the

music. Of course, that is when I do not have a job on a Sunday morning."
The social and political impact of the mike men, therefore, was remarkable as they sought to get their messages into areas that were not accessible to radio and other forms of public information. They communicated with the people, lived among them and played their music for their enjoyment. As with other aspects of their routines, the constant playing of Indian film songs kept those songs alive among the people, and in time, the songs became commonplace among them, and the mike men gained in status among East Indians. Announcements, however, remain the mainstay of income for many regular mike men.

Mike men showing support at a funeral service of one of their colleagues.

A mike men Sound-off competition in full swing

CHAPTER 7

Identity Markers

Even as the mike man went about his business earning an income, he unwittingly made a tremendous contribution to the popularity of Indian film songs and the exhibition of Indian movies. This helped in creating an East Indian identity for East Indians linked to Indian films and Indian film songs.

While the mike men began their journey in Trinidad as entrepreneurs, their mike playing routines aided in the evolution of East Indian culture and identity in the country. Whether they played their music as a hobby or as hired agents, their impact on East Indians was phenomenal. They became identified with Indian film music, which formed the core of an evolving East Indian identity in Trinidad. They were hired for announcements of Indian movies at cinemas, and played Indian film songs at weddings and Hindu religious occasions.

In the early days of the cinema in Trinidad (1900-1945), advertisements were usually done using storefront windows, posters at strategic locations, distribution of flyers by hired flyer-boys, and newspaper advertisements. Most cinemas were located in urban areas and depended mainly on the walk-in crowd since transportation to and from outlying districts posed difficulties in terms of costs and availability at nighttime. Before the advent of Indian movies in 1935, East Indians were not known to frequent cinemas. Cinema owners, to encourage East Indians to leave their comfort zone and attend the cinema in urban areas, sent flyer-boys into the villages to distribute flyers announcing the arrival of a new movie. They left flyers at shops, doctors' offices, schools, and other places. Also, posters were stuck up at the village shops and other locations, but these had limited success since many East Indians could neither read nor write in the English language. Ramesh Boodhoo, a former cinema owner, indicated that with the development of the Indian film industry in this country, cinema owners needed to find a different way to get their messages to East Indians, and this was where the mike men made a significant contribution.

Beginning in the late 1940s, cinema owners exhibiting Indian movies employed the services of the mike men who went into the rural areas to advertise Indian films. Boodhoo also indicated that every cinema that exhibited Indian movies had a mike man attached to it. Sometimes, depending on the popularity of the movie and the songs, and the size of the area to be covered by the announcements, three or four mikes were hired by the same cinema owner to go into the surrounding areas to advertise the movie. Some cinemas had three or four mike men attached to them for regular announcements while a few actually owned one or two mike systems.

The mike men went into the predominantly East Indian villages and publicized Indian movies in a manner that no other medium could match. Their remit was to attract East Indians to the cinema, and this they did creditably playing songs from the soon to be released film during the advertising journey. In the same manner in which people ran out of their homes to see and listen to the mike when it journeyed to the 'cooking night' house or when it 'carried' the wedding, they came out and stood by the roadside when they heard the 'cinema' announcements.

In advertising the Indian movie, the mike man played Indian film songs as a beacon call to attention, then cut into the song still playing softly in the background and spoke of the Indian movie being shown in the nearby cinemas. He drove through the villages very slowly, attracting maximum attention because of the sheer loudness of the music being played. As he drove along, he distributed flyers relating to the Indian movie being shown. Many people were encouraged to attend the exhibition of the film at the cinema, mainly because of the work of the mike man playing the songs from the movie as he advertised it. In like manner, Jagroopsingh pointed out that "we were eager to hear the mike man play the songs from the movies and this was a great motivation for us to see the movies," while Sitahal added that without the work of the mike men publicizing Indian movies in the villages, cinemas would have been hard-pressed to get a decent crowd for Indian films. He further mentioned that people "remembered the songs that were played on the mike, and it kept 'ringing in our minds, ears'; it seemed to cast a spell upon us, and until we saw the movie, we were not satisfied."

By playing the film songs from Indian movies at several hired occasions, the mike man unknowingly encouraged the process whereby they were identified with Indian film songs, and East Indians also identified with the Indian film songs. Even as the mike man went about his business earning an income, he unwittingly made a tremendous contribution to the popularity of Indian film songs and the exhibition of Indian movies. This helped in creating an East Indian identity for East Indians linked to Indian films and Indian film songs. In those early years before the advent of Indian movies in Trinidad, the average East Indian was starved of Indian music and songs. The only source of songs and music for them was the mike man who endeared himself to the villagers with the playing of popular songs from Indian movies, whether it was during roving announcements or at the cooking nights. There was a natural link between Indian film songs, the mike man and the people. Eventually, people associated the mike man with Indian film songs. Later, Indian film songs became an identity symbol for East Indians in the 1950s and 60s, and it was during that period that there was a crystallization of Indian film songs connecting to East Indian identity. (Gooptar, 2012).[34]

The influence of the mike man also extended to several religious functions among the East Indians, particularly among the Hindus, where he also played Indian film songs, but this time his repertoire was limited to spiritual songs from Indian movies. The cumulative effect of the mike men constantly bombarding East Indians with Indian film songs popularized those songs among them in a manner that had not been achieved by the traditional songs that existed in the East Indian communities. Narsaloo Ramaya (interview 2008) argued that

34   see The Impact of Indian movies on East Indian identity in Trinidad, 2012, by Primnath Gooptar for more details on this topic.

Indian film songs gradually replaced traditional folk and religious songs at East Indian events. He noted that the average East Indian had been starved of any new identity connections with India, and Indian movies were seen as an identity connection with India. The songs were catchy, rhythmic, and 'modern' in the eyes of most East Indians who generally preferred to listen to the filmi songs rather than the traditional East Indian songs. In time, due to the work of the mike men, Indian film songs became an identity icon among the East Indians.

By the mid-1950s, mike men had also become an indispensable part of the success of major Hindu religious activities in the Indian settlement communities. For example, his contribution was a significant input to the success in the hosting of community Ramayan Yaagnas, Bhagwat Yaagnas, monthly Kathas, Ramleela celebrations, and Phagwa celebrations. Also, the mike men's input played a significant role in the success of community sporting events, bazaars, and some parties. His contributions were generally in three areas: announcing the event, providing a microphone for the speakers such as pundits at religious ceremonies and the announcers at sports meetings, and playing relevant music for the occasion. With Hindu religious events such as Ramayan Yaagnas and Bhagwat Yaagnas, the mike man arrived early at the location, by 5 pm, and played religious songs from Indian films. This, Sitahal suggested, was a wake-up call for villagers, reminding them that the yaagna was in progress and would begin shortly that evening. Many people came early merely to listen to the religious songs played by the mike men. In the case of sports meetings, the mike was an indispensable part of the proceedings as the announcer kept everyone abreast of what was happening on the sports field above the noisy crowd. This was possible because of the wide reach of the horns and its loudness, which could be heard above the noise on the sports ground. Besides, whenever there was a lull in the proceedings, the mike man always filled in the gaps by playing Indian film songs.

In these scenarios, it must be noted that while he was hired for various types of announcements, the mike man played Indian film songs in public spaces and unwittingly claimed those public spaces for East Indians. This consumption of Indian film songs by East Indians in public spaces added significantly to the other occasions when the mike man played Indian film songs, and the cumulative effect was one of East Indian identity with Indian film songs.

Indian movie songs provided the perfect platform for the growth and development of the mike men in Trinidad from the 1950s to the 1960s when they were considered to be in their heydays. This period also coincided with the Golden Era of Indian cinema, when some of the most melodious songs were produced in India for Indian movies. The Indian film producers, music directors, and playback singers produced their films and songs primarily for Indian audiences in India and surrounding countries. None of them had an inkling that in this tiny colony of Trinidad, there lived over 300,000 Indians and that their movies and songs were having a significant impact on the people of Trinidad and Tobago and other islands in the Caribbean such as Guyana and Surinam. But the vinyl 78 RPM records made their way to Trinidad, and in the hands of the mike man, those songs helped to create a cultural renaissance among East Indians.

No other film industry in the world, whose films were shown on the island, had such an impact on local groups as Indian film songs had on the East Indians in this country in that era. While many films made in America, England, France, and China were shown locally, they did not have a similar effect on any other segment of the local population such as the Chinese, Portuguese, French, Afro Trinidadians, as the Indian movies, songs, and music had on the East Indians. A significant part of that impact on the local community was because of the work of the mike men's use of filmi songs and the manner in which they performed their duties with their vital stock in trade, 78 RPM vinyl records.

Cultural Influence

Wherever he went, up to the 1970s, the mike man was a veritable star boy; he was the man of the moment, almost given celebrity status. Everyone wanted to know him, to meet him, to talk to him or just to be around him. People in villages where the mike man gave his services talked for days afterward about meeting him, talking to him, nodding to him, or merely listening to the film songs he played. Those who requested songs he played, spoke about the event for weeks afterward.

Ramsumair noted.," the mike man in Trinidad was a great asset to the development of Indian culture, especially Indian film songs and cooking nights. They helped to build and keep alive a unique tradition of Indian film songs being played on the road, at Indian weddings and other special events such as bazaars and sports meetings in the rural areas of the country. The mike men must be commended for the tremendous job they did and continue to do regarding the playing of Indian film songs and upkeep of Indian culture in this country."

The mike men were largely responsible for the spread and development of Indian film songs in Trinidad and Tobago. They are the repository of the most extensive collection of Indian film songs in the country. They are collectors of old and rare Indian film songs, which are considered prized possessions. There are Indian film songs in the possession of mike men that are never heard on the radio. It was the mike man who in the early days before the advent of radio, took Indian film songs to the people in the outlying areas, particularly in the Indian settlement areas: they were the ones who kept it alive among the East Indian people and who provided a voice for the East Indians. The mike man's job was a labour of love in the early days of the mike in Trinidad because the financial return from the letting of the mike system was minimal. He provided musical enjoyment for East Indians while giving a voice to East Indian identity in public spaces. The public, in turn, held him in high esteem and, in time, saw him as a cultural icon among them.

Some mike men shared the view that a special museum should be established to further preserve the legacy of the mike men of Trinidad.

Mike Museum

Ricky Harrypersad, a young man with a heart of gold expressed a wish to preserve the traditions of the mike men:
"I admire what you are trying to do in this book, and that is to record the history of the mike men and to preserve that history for posterity. I share your

thoughts and aspirations in trying to preserve the legacy of the mike men. Most of the earlier mike men are gone and forgotten. For some time now, I've also been thinking about ways and means of preserving the legacy of the mike man, and I would like to spearhead an effort to establish a Mike Museum somewhere in this country for the public and young people in particular to visit and educate themselves about the mike men of Trinidad."

This author commended Harrypersad for his keen interest in preserving the heritage of the mike men and suggested that an approach to the National Council of Indian Culture (NCIC) and the NCIC Heritage Center might be a step in the right direction in furthering that idea. He indicated to Harrypersad that there was merit in the suggestion, and with support, such a project could come to fruition.

On the topic of the Museum, Anderson noted, "the NCIC is the best place to house such a museum because that is where this sound-off competition began way back in the 1990s. When it started then, it was called the Mike-o-Rama competition, but after a few years, the competition ceased as the NCIC had put a complete ban on the use of alcohol and meat on the compound. I would be willing to work with the Mike Men Association and the NCIC in the establishment of this center, and I can provide some artifacts for that Museum, and I'm sure that other mike men would contribute likewise."

Randy Kissoon, joining the discussion added, "I am in full agreement with the establishment of a Mike Museum at the NCIC if a place can be allocated for us to set up our equipment and other apparatus so that people can see and touch the mike system of long ago and today. Many of us have in our possession components of the mike system that can be donated. Many young people do not know what a 78 RPM Record looks like so these and other Mike items can be displayed there.

"I am sure that the Mike Men Association will support this move, and we will assist in curating that aspect of the NCIC Heritage Center. We would be delighted to contribute to this and to make it happen. Perhaps something like this can be done in time for the launch of this book when the book is completed next year."

On the same topic, Basdeo added, "if the mike men Museum becomes a reality, I would also like to see, in some part of that Museum, a listing of all the mike men in Trinidad and Tobago, both past and present. It could be as a kind of Hall of Fame for the Mike men, particularly for those who have passed on, with their photos, their mike systems, and the names on their mike systems. For example, if a mike man called Lal Singh (deceased) owned a mike system which he called the *Hawk*, that could be noted on the wall or some aspect of the Heritage Center's Mike Museum with a picture of him and the image of the mike system *Hawk* and a brief history of the individual."

Conclusion

The mike men played a significant role in the evolution of East Indian identity in Trinidad because of their (the mike men's) influence on the social, cultural, and religious events among East Indians. Their constant playing of Indian film songs pushed into the background East Indian traditional songs and music and etched into the psyche of the East Indian, the 'modern' Indian film songs of the 1950s and 60s. East Indians embraced the new type of Indian filmi music and gave high status to the mike men and treated them like stars in the communities.

The mike men, in turn, brought East Indians closer to India through the Indian filmi music they played. There was a definite affinity between the Indian film songs and East Indians in Trinidad. During the period under discussion, East Indians in Trinidad struggled to claim their space in the country, and the mike men's playing Indian filmi songs substantially contributed to their claiming a space in this land. East Indians identified with the Indian film songs because it provided a link to their ancestral homeland, India.

For many people, the mike men will always have a special place in their lives because of the tremendous contribution they made to East Indian culture and the evolution of East Indian identity in Trinidad. Without the work of the mike men, Indian film songs would not have been as popular and widespread as they were in the 1950s, 60s, and 70s. It is the work of the mike men that kept Indian film songs popular among the East Indian communities, and it was this popularity of Indian film songs that eventually led to the identification of East Indians with Indian film songs and their spin-offs. Whenever a cultural item reflecting East Indian tradition was required for a public program, usually, an Indian film song was selected.

During the period under consideration, the mike men were the gatekeepers of Indian culture and Indian film songs in the country. Wherever they went, they played their stock in trade; Indian film songs and thereby kept Indian culture alive among East Indians. The playing of Indian film songs by the mike men in the streets of the country, at cooking nights, weddings, and in public spaces, helped to build the self-esteem of East Indians who hitherto practiced their religion and culture in privacy. East Indians were not known to broadcast their culture and religion in public spaces, but the coming of the mike men changed that, and for the first time, Indian songs were played regularly in public areas for all to hear. The claiming of the public space by the mike men encouraged East Indians to boldly assert themselves at a time when they were struggling to claim an identity in Trinidad, an identity that was indelibly linked to Indian film songs. The mike men epitomized for many East Indians the keepers of their culture in the country, and they collectively preserved one of the tangible heritages of the East Indians in Trinidad, Indian film songs.

Since Indian film songs aided East Indians in their identity formation and the mike men were the ones who brought the Indian film songs to the people and kept it alive among them, they were held in high esteem by the people and, with time, they became cultural icons in the East Indian community.

As beloved cultural icons, they continued upholding a great local tradition, an indigenous tradition they had created in this country. The work of the mike men over the years has been preserved in the memories of several generations as captured in this book. Their iconic artistry of playing mike at cooking nights, weddings and through the villages is indigenous to this country and the mike men deserve to be called cultural icons in this country. What they created remains indigenous to Trinidad, and they should be honoured for their work over the years.

A mike man poses with his portable record player and a 78 RPM Record

CHAPTER 8

THE MIKE AND THE MIKE MEN IN PICTURES

MEMBERS OF THE MIKE MEN ASSOCIATION OF TRINIDAD AND TOBAGO

The Executive

PRESIDENT

Name: **Anand Kissoon**
Address: Perseverance Road, Chandernagore, Chaguanas.

VICE PRESIDENT

Name: **Anand Boxer**
Address: Esperanza Village, California.

SECRETARY

Name: **Jeevan Gary Dassawh**
Address: 12 Lothians Branch Road, Princes Town.

ASSISTANT SECRETARY

Name: **Shaheed Mohammed**
Address: #35 Seuradge Trace, Penal.

TREASURER

Name: **Gopaul Ramsamooj**
Address: #30 St John's Trace
            Avocat, Fyzabad.

PUBLIC RELATIONS OFFICER

Name: **Premnath Ramnath**
Address: 11a Carolina # 1 Trace,
            Carolina Village, Couva.

Name: **Randy Kissoon**
Address: # 60 Ramsingh Street,
            Munroe Road, Cunupia

Former president of the Trinidad and Tobago Mobile Paging Association

Mike Men in Pictures

Name:
Dhanraj Ramboodh

Address:
109 Sinnanan St.
Kelly Village, Caroni.

Name:
Shafeer Mohammed

Address:
Preysal Ground Trace,
Chicken Road, Freeport.

Name:
Bissoon Persad

Address:
LP 60 of Lime Road,
Chase Village,
Carapichaima.

Name:
Rodney Mahabir

Address:
LP 249 Malgretoute
Junction,
Princes Town.

Name:
Krishendath Ramdeo

Address:
Couva.

Name:
Kenrick Ramnarace

Address:
Mattanlal Trace,
St Magrit Village,
Claxton Bay.

Mike Men in Pictures

Name:
Haytram Ramdass

Address:
LP 104 Calcutta Road #1,
Mc Bean Village, Couva.

Name:
Latchman Bhagwandeen

Address:
Southern Main Road,
Chase Village,
Carapichaima.

Name:
Ramnarine Ramourtar

Address:
92 Thompson Road,
Palmiste.

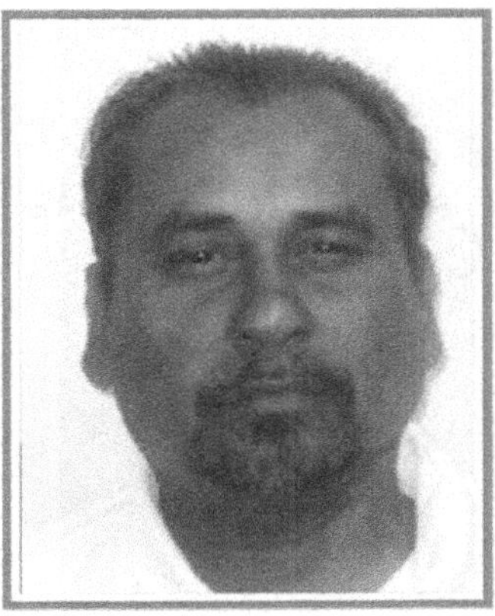

Name:
Kishore Samlal

Address:
206 Tarouba Road,
Marabella.

Name:
Lalla Ramsaroop

Address:
37 St Julien Road,
Princess Town.

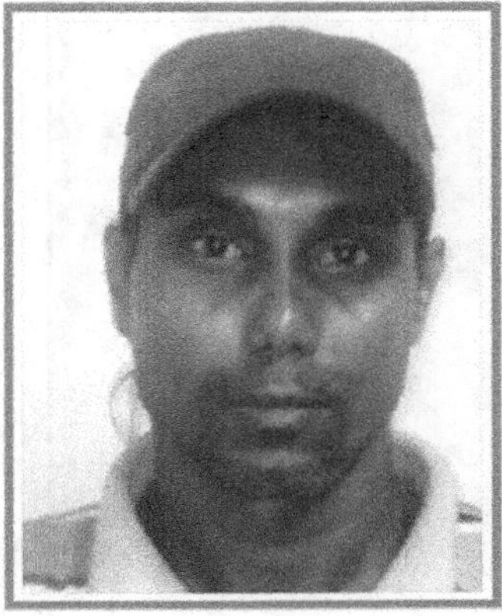

Name:
Mahendralal Sookoo

Address:
Sookoo Trace,
Espranza Village,
California.

Mike Men in Pictures

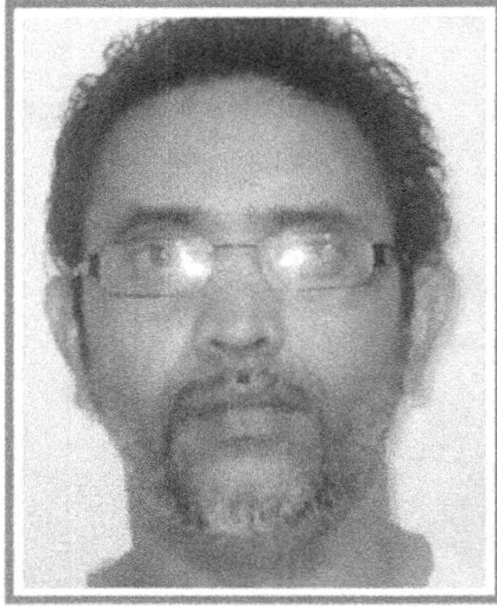

Name:
**Ramcharan
Rambaran**

Address:
LP # 4 Jerningham
Junction,
Cunupia.

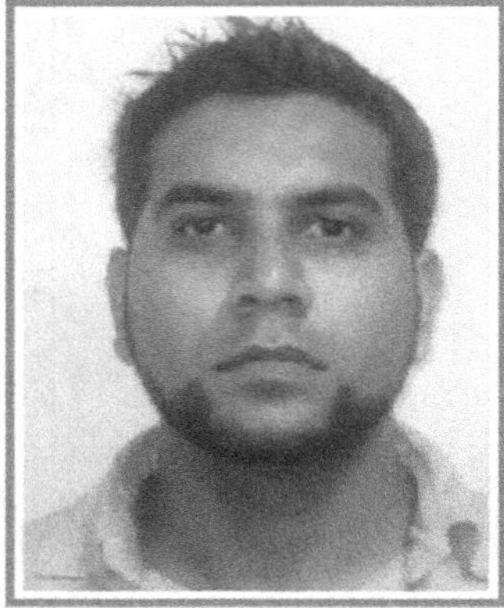

Name:
**Vinod Persad
Maharaj**

Address:
Coromandel Village,
Cedros.

Name:
Bansraj Harry

Address:
7 Moore Trace,
Cunupia.

Name:
Amar Ramsaran

Address:
#74-10 School Street,
Esperanza Village.

Name:
Jagit Ramrattan

Address:
#136 Ackbar Trace,
Siparia Old Road,
Fyzabad.

Name:
Ramsaran Bhola

Address:
Ragbir Street, Dinsley
Village, Tacarigua.

Mike Men in Pictures

Name:
Siewnanan Ram

Address:
Esmerelda Road,
Cunupia.

Name:
Balraj Boodram

Address:
37 Lawrence Wong
Road,
Enterprise, Chaguanass.

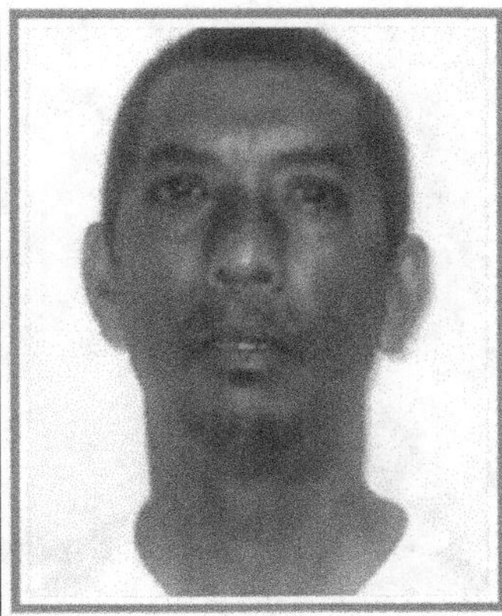

Name:
Rahim Ramjohn

Address:
Perseverance, Couva.

Name:
Goberdhan Jaglal

Address:
LP 31 Ragoonanan
Road, Enterprise,
Chaguanas.

Name:
Samrally Ali

Address:
Rees Road,
Barrackpore.

Name:
Krishna Teemol

Address:
#9 Ramraj Ave.,
Mohess Road, Debe.

Mike Men in Pictures

Name:
Sahadeo Magram

Address:
Cupunia.

Name:
Sukhdeo Pitiram

Address:
22 Dinoo Road,
Challieville, Chaguanas.

Name:
**Jankie Persad
Mangaru**

Address:
#7 Endeavour Road,
Chaguanas.

Name:
Suresh Kissoon

Address:
#71 Forres Park Road,
Claxton Bay.

Name:
Dipchan Siewnarine

Address:
#29 Gath Road, Princes
Town.
Deceased 6/02/16

Name:
**Kishore Persad
Maharaj**

Address:
Coromandel Village,
Cedros.

Mike Men in Pictures

Name:
Deonanan Kishore

Address:
4 Daniel Private Road,
Darneaud Street,
Gasparillo.

Name:
Dennis Kishore

Address:
#4 Daniel Pr. Road,
Darneaud Street,
Gasparillo.

Name:
Chanbally Jagmohan

Address:
81 Cedar Hill Road,
Princes Town.

Name:
Mahabir Siewnarine

Address:
39 Cuchawan Trace
West, Debe.

Name:
Sudesh Sooknanan

Address:
46 Digity Village,
Debe.

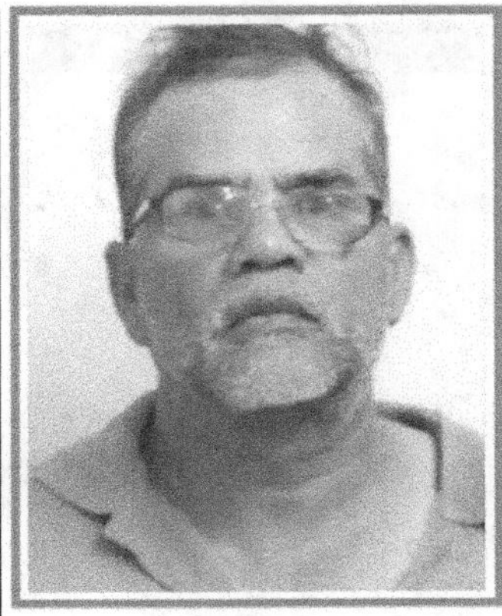

Name:
**Tillbenny Francis
Garib**

Address:
9 New Settlement,
Dow Village.

Mike Men in Pictures

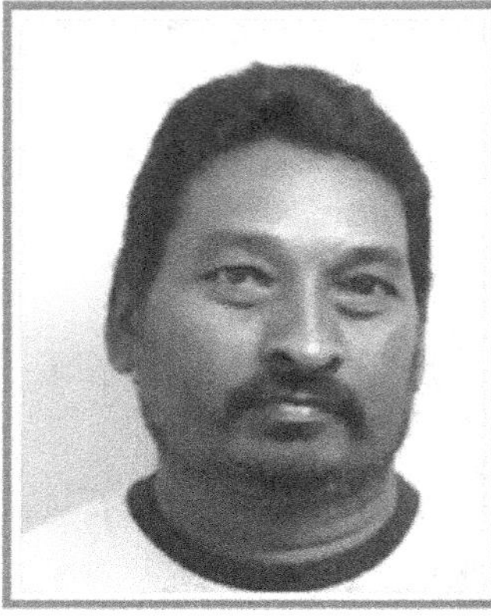

Name:
Ganger-Persad Beharry

Address:
San Francique, Penal.

Name:
Teerath Kanhai

Address:
2 Spring Drive Crown Trace, Enterprise, Chaguanas.

Name:
Dipchand Deonarine

Address:
2mm Depot Road, Longdenville, Chaguanas.

Name:
Seenath Persad

Address:
Palmyra Village, Princes Town.

Name:
Rajendra David Gosine

Address:
19 Paradise Avenue, California.

Name:
Ramkrishna Bhagoutie

Address:
LP # 59 Bamboo Settlement, Valsayn.

Mike Men in Pictures

Name:
Khamraj Chotkana

Address:
51 Kolahal Road,
Charlieville,
Chaguanas.

Name:
Rakesh Boodram

Address:
#37 Lawrence Wong
Road,
Enterprise.

Name:
Pooran Banmalie

Address:
21a Sookoo Trace,
Claxton Bay.

Name:
**Churaman
Ramkissoon**

Address:
Kallian Road, Las
Lomas No 1.

Name:
Ramlochan Ramdeo

Address:
 #124 Batchyia Trace,
Penal.

Name:
Moonlal Ramkissoon

Address:
Las Lomas No 1,
Las Lomas.

Mike Men in Pictures

Name:
Sandesh Gajadhar

Address:
#308 Macaulay
Junction, Claxton Bay

Name:
Kelvin Gajadhar

Address:
#308 Macaulay
Junction, Claxton Bay.

Name:
Wazid Ali

Address:
LP 21 First Street W,
Beaulieu Ave.,
Trincity.

Name:
Imtiaz Omar Ali

Address:
3 Fifth Street,
Barataria

Name:
Partap Kuarsingh

Address:
LP 20 Lalbeharry Trace,
Debe.
Deceased

Name:
Keshan Ramsamooj

Address:
45 St John Trace,
Avocat,
Fyzabad.

Mike Men in Pictures

Name:
Indarjit Heralal

Address:
Southern Main Road,
Mc Bean, Couva.

Name:
Daren P. Emmanuel

Address:
161 Tarouba Road,
Marabella.

Name:
Charles Armoogam

Address:
213 Golconda Village,
Cipero Road.
San Fernando.

Name:
Charan Ramsamooj

Address:
St John Trace, Avocat,
Fyzabad.

Name:
Baldath Jugmohan

Address:
Papourie Road,
Barackpore.

Name:
Dilip Debiram

Address:
Moore Trace, Bejucal.

Mike Men in Pictures

Name:
Boughnarine Basdeo

Address:
Lot 79 Dyette Estate,
Cunupia.

Name:
Shashi Boodram

Address:
Munroe Road, Cunupia.

Name:
Sharaz Khan

Address:
381 Aripero Village,
Rousillac.

Name:
**Harrypersad
Harrikissoon**

Address:
New York, USA.

Name:
Sais Moonilal

Address:
Gasparillo.

Name:
Moses

Address:
Penal.

Mike Men in Pictures

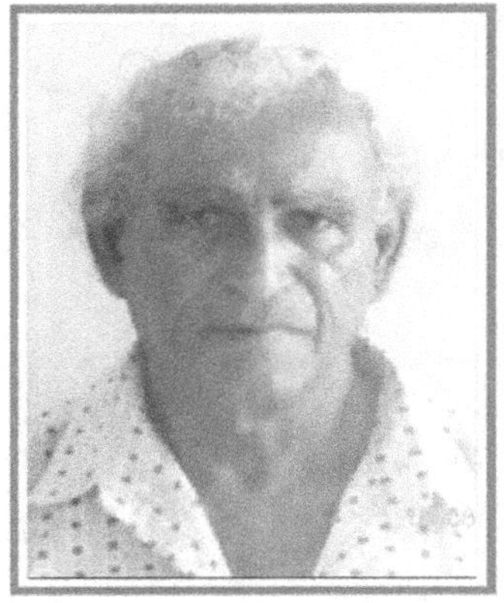

Name:
Chaitnath L. Babadeen

Address:
#19 Antilies Trace, San Francique, Penal.

Name:
Rajendra Babadeen

Address:
19 Antilies Trace, San Francique, Penal

Name:
Ajodha Kuarsingh (Anil)

Address:
LP 208 Lalbeharry Trace, Debe.

Name:
Joe

Address:
USA.

MIKE MEN: WINNERS AND TROPHIES

MIKE MEN SOUND-OFF COMPETITIONS

BIBLIOGRAPHY

Gooptar, Primnath. The Impact of Indian Movies on East Indian Identity in Trinidad. Ph.D. Dissertation. UTT. 2012.

Interviewees

Anderson Bahaw, 30, Technician, lives in Cunupia, Trinidad. He has been in the mike business from a young age as his father and uncles owned mike systems and he went with them as they played at various venues.

Balliram Ramoutar, (1939 --) a mike man with over 50 years' experience in the business. He has trained several young people in the mike business. Couva.

Darren Basdeo, 40, Truck driver, and resides in Longdenville, Chaguanas. He was born into a family of mike men and grew up with it, going out with the mike men from an early age.

Dianand Balgobin, 39, Works at Ministry of Agriculture and hails from Tableland, Princes Town. He has been a mike man for over 25 years, having been born into a family that owned mike systems.

Dipchand Maharaj, Deceased. 92, retired school supervisor, St. Augustine.

Doeraj Harrikissoon, 94, retired Sugar Cane worker, Palmyra Village.

Harrypersad Harrikissoon, 62, mike man, USA and Trinidad. Returns periodically to participate in the sound-of gatherings and competitions.

Hublal Ramkissoon, (1949....) is a religious and cultural activist and the owner of two mike systems. He is self-employed and repairs mike systems as a hobby. He has over 40 years' experience as a mike man. His father was a mike man and he retains two mike systems used by his father in the 1940s and 50s. Rio Claro.

Ishmael Hoosaney now resides in Canada but returns home regularly to participate in the mike men sound-off gatherings and competitions. He played mike in Trinidad for over 30 years before migrating to Canada but keeps in touch with the mike fraternity in this country.

James Ramnath (1910-1909) was a former educator and retired principal of the Cumuto CM (now Presbyterian) school. He spoke extensively at Indian Arrival functions in Sangre Grande and environs and was considered very knowledgeable in matters relating to East Indians in Trinidad. Sangre Grande.

John Jagroopsingh, 78, retired tractor driver, Arima Race Track. Brazil Village, Arima.   (Deceased)

Krishna Timol, 56, Welder/fabricator and lives in Penal. He has been playing mike for as long as he could remember, having been born into a family of mike men. From an early age, he accompanied his father and uncles when they went out to play mike at weddings and other places.

Mulchan Singh, 79, retired farmer, Princes Town.

Nanlal Ramcharan (1910--2016) was a retired farmer, cultural and religious activist. He grew up in Plum Road with his parents Jagrani (mother) and Ramcharan Singh who both came from India. He was considered very knowledgeable on the East Indian presence in Trinidad. Plum Road, Sangre Grande.

Narsaloo Ramaya (1919 –2013) was an accomplished violinist and considered a pioneer in Indian music and culture in Trinidad. He was the leader of the Naya Zamana Indian Orchestra from 1967 to 1976 and was awarded the Hummingbird Bronze Medal (1970) for culture. He is considered very knowledgeable about Indian culture and Indian music. San Juan.

Partap Sitahal, (1946----) is a retired Machine Operator. He is Vice President, Brazil Hindu Temple, and is a community, cultural, religious, and political activist. He is very knowledgeable about Indian movies and the mike men in Trinidad. Brazil Village, Arima.

Pickrani Gooptar, 72, San Rafael, Arima. Housewife.

Ralph Narine (1922—2017), was a former magistrate and retired judge and Indian cultural activist. He played music with the S. M. Aziz group in 1930s before the group was transformed into an Indian orchestra. Narine was considered very knowledgeable in Indian culture and Indian music. Port of Spain.

Ramdeowar Ramjattan, (1920- 2012) was a retired Caroni worker and mike man. He had over 60 years' experience as a mike man. St. Augustine.

Ramesh Boodoo, (1941- 2016) was a former cinema owner/operator who spent most of his adult life in the cinema business. He owned and operated the Silk cinema in Sangre Grande and regularly interacted with the mike men of his area. Sangre Grande.

Randy Kissoon, (1954-) … is self-employed and the owner of three mike systems. A former president of the Trinidad and Tobago Mobile Paging Association. He has over 30 years' experience in the mike business. Cunupia.

Ranjit Singh, 94, retired sugar cane worker, Penal.

Ricky Harrypersad, 40, mike man, Couva. Has been a mike man from a young age.

Rooplal Boodlal, 67, a retiree, has been a mike man for six years. He resides in Barrackpore.

Shaheed Mohammed, Assistant Secretary, Mike Men Association of T&T, Penal.

Siew Gosein, (1918- 2010). Male. 91 years. Retired labourer. Mike man enthusiast and former Indar Sabha Dancer and Raja Harischandra dance drama artiste (1930s -1960s)

Siew Lalchan, 88, retired farmer, Cedros.

Sonia Maharaj, 95, retired Sugar Cane worker, Rio Claro.

BOOKS BY THE SAME AUTHOR